What people are saying about "Think Differently Live Differently"

"In this book you will find the simple yet deep truths to the freedom that so often eludes us. Be ready to be challenged and encouraged to walk in the fullness of who you truly are in God. Bob Hamp exposes lifelong lies we've all allowed ourselves to believe and helps us to see the truth. A life changing book!"

— Kari Jobe, Dove Award Winning Artist

"I have personally benefitted from Bob Hamp's revelatory teaching and anointed ministry. God has gifted him with the ability to articulate powerful Kingdom truths in a manner that is easy to understand and to put into practice. This powerful book Bob has written is a must read for every believer desiring greater freedom, fulfillment and intimacy with God."

— Jimmy Evans, President of "Marriage Today"

"Bob Hamp has dedicated his life as a pastor and mentor to helping people pursue lasting freedom. This book is a great resource built on his years of experience. It communicates life-changing principles using parables, word pictures and real life illustrations, pointing each of us to the thing we are all searching for: true freedom."

— Dr. Caroline Leaf, Bestselling Author of Who Switched off My Brain

"Bob Hamp has clear insight into a very complex topic. This book is for every person who wants to understand the kingdom of God and the freedom found only in Christ."

— Brady Boyd, Senior Pastor of New Life Church in Colorado Springs

"Bob Hamp has nailed it. With riveting analogies, unique humor and incredible biblical insight and understanding, he has brought to light, in an easy to understand way, what most people are fearful of exploring. This book helped me tremendously and is a must read for anyone seeking release and freedom from the chains of their past, and desiring to move on to better and brighter things in their life."

— Mike Brisky, 7 year PGA Tour Veteran

THINK
DIFFERENTLY
LIVE
DIFFERENTLY

KEYS TO A LIFE OF FREEDOM

THINK DIFFERENTLY LIVE DIFFERENTLY

KEYS TO A LIFE OF FREEDOM

BOB HAMP

Unless otherwise stated, all Scriptures quotations are taken from the New American Standard Holy Bible.

ISBN 978-1-4507-0920-0 North American edition

ISBN 978-1-907080-09-8 International edition

Library of Congress Control Number: 2010926650

Visit http://bobhamp.com for blog and further ministry information

Distributed outside of North America by Integrity Media Europe

Printed in the United States of America

Acknowledgements

There is nothing new under the sun, and as I have written this book, I have become increasingly aware of the truth of this. Anything of worth I may contribute, I have received from someone, somewhere at some time. I never set out to become an expert on freedom, I just wanted to avoid falling into the traps of those who went before me.

Thanks to my Father in Heaven for reaching out to me through His Son, Jesus and rescuing me again and again from myself, and all the things that have entangled me. Thanks to His Holy Spirit for empowering a life I never would have imagined.

I am grateful for…

— countless mentors and teachers who have paid the price to think differently and to do so out loud in front of people. Men and women who have influenced me simply by pursuing their own wholeness.

— Brad Bankhead who set my feet on a course of knowing God, and finding Him to be powerful and pertinent in every moment.

— My mother who, in searching for her own path, gave me the freedom to search as well.

— David McQueen, the Senior Pastor of Beltway Park and to all the Elders there who gave me a place of real healing and real friendship.

— My Pastor Robert Morris, who has also given me a great deal of freedom to pursue freedom for myself, and for all who will engage.

— John Sandford for both the time, and genuine love that he shared with me at a time when I was in need.

I am especially grateful to …

— the best mother-in-law in the world, Jettie Omdahl, who not only fed me and cleaned up after me as I wrote, but she also read, edited, pushed and pulled to help birth the first manuscript of this book.

— Amy Cook, whose skill, passion and integrity brought richness and clarity to my writing.

— And Tim Pettingale for reaching out to a stranger across the ocean and turning a rough manuscript into a book.

— Thanks to the greatest kids in the world, Ian, Jillian, Jenna, and Atticus, who allowed me to put many hours into learning and writing the concepts found in these pages.

— Last but in no way least, I am grateful to my wife, Jackee, who lived with me and drew out of me the story of freedom, and then endured the process while I poured hours (or years) into the actual writing of this thing.

Table of Contents

Foreword

*Have you ever felt like you know who you're supposed to be –
you're just not very good at it?*

From the moment I started Gateway Church, I had a vision! A vision to not only see people saved, but set free. I decided we needed something that, until then, I had never heard of or seen anywhere else. We needed a "Freedom Pastor". I searched the world over to find a pastor who knew how to help people find and walk in the freedom Jesus died to give us. I searched for a man who loved God, his family, and people; who was biblically balanced and who was, quite frankly, not goofy! The person I found was Bob Hamp. Bob is a man who knows God and His Word; a man who loves God and His people; a man who knows the secrets and the steps to get free and walk in freedom.

Within a few months of Bob's arrival, I was encouraging the whole church to go through the new Freedom Ministry program which had been created. Hundreds signed up and Bob and his team began to teach and minister to them. Shortly after, testimonies of changed lives began to stream in. People who had suffered from persistent abuse got healed. People struggling with addictions were set free. People who came from a legalistic, religious background were released to walk in joy and victory. It was amazing! And the testimonies continue to flood in to this day.

Since Jesus died to make us free, why is it that so many of us are not free? Why do so many things hold us in bondage and keep us from being the overcoming Christians that we desire to be? What did we lose in the garden when Adam sinned? What was restored to us when

Jesus came back from the dead? If, as the Bible says, the truth sets us free, why aren't we experiencing that freedom to a greater degree? What are the obstacles that need to be removed for us to become the people God created us to be?

Help is at hand. In this book Bob explores all these issues and more. The conclusion? You *can* become the person God created you to be, no matter what you have been through or are still struggling with.

I know what it's like to be "saved" and yet still be in bondage. I know what it's like to be a slave to past hurts and insecurities. But by God's grace, I also know what it's like to be set free. True freedom – to be ourselves as God intended – really is possible here and now. In this book, Bob clearly shows us the path to freedom. He teaches us not just how to think different thoughts, but how to *think differently* and, as a result, how to *live differently*. As you work through the principles contained within, your personal route to freedom will emerge and you will leave the bondage of the past behind.

The next testimony that needs to be shared is yours. You really can be the person God created you to be. Freedom is not learning to be someone or something else; it is simply learning to become *who you really are*. There is hope! Read on and learn how to take hold of your freedom now.

Robert Morris
Senior Pastor, Gateway Church
Bestselling author of *The Blessed Life*

Part One

THINK
DIFFERENTLY

The Journey Begins

Why Did He Go?

I can still see her face as she answered my question. The stress on her countenance faded into a faraway look as if she were in a trance. It seemed as though she had suddenly left on a vacation without moving from the chair in front of me. The lines around her eyes softened and the look of fear and frustration momentarily melted. Having mentally arrived at her new destination, she was ready to answer me.

I had been working as a juvenile probation officer for a few years. This, like many other meetings, took place in a moment of crisis. The strands of life this single mother had been holding together were unraveling fast and she viewed me as another agent of fear in her life. What would happen to her son? Would she lose him to long term detention or any one of multiple placement options? Like so many other parents, she came to my office swimming in a sea of competing emotions.

She had come to pick up her son who had stolen her car and run away from home. After a frantic period of waiting and searching, he had been located several states away – Florida, if I remember correctly. Out of gas and out of resources, he had left a trail of forged credit card receipts. After many attempts to fill up and drive-off, the boy had finally been picked up, claimed by his mom and returned to our small West Texas town. Now she was sitting in the sterile office, wondering what this probation officer was going to do and trying to figure out her next step. We had established the basic information about his age, family background and the nature of their relationship, but I was still curious – why Florida? Was her son running to family, friends, or even a girlfriend who had moved out of state? So I asked the question: "Ma'am," I said, "why did he choose Florida? Is there someone there he knew?"

This was the question that had prompted the shift in her body language. Her eyes narrowed and looked as if she were scanning the horizon in my diminutive office. Her imagination departed on the journey, although part of her remained behind to answer me. "Why Florida?" she repeated, "I wasn't sure either until I went to pick him up. But the further I drove and the further Texas fell behind me, the more I began to understand." She paused, eyes still distant, "We don't know anyone there, and I am not even sure if he knew exactly where he was hoping to get to … but having driven the same way, I know exactly why he went." She seemed to have reached that faraway destination as she summed up her explanation in a single word, laden with emotional significance to her. As she uttered the word, it seemed weighty enough to reach beyond her and her son to include all of us.

"Freedom," she answered. "He went for *freedom*. The further I traveled, it was as if I was leaving behind every care and every difficulty. The more I drove, the more I considered joining him, because life just seemed easier in front of me than it did behind me."

Like her son, she had a picture of freedom in her mind. This picture, however inaccurate, would point her heart towards the pursuit of freedom. His picture had been so skewed that his greatest bid for release had actually resulted in the loss of all his freedoms.

Our brief conversation had already revealed that her life had been long and difficult. Many painful experiences had clouded her past and led up to this one. This day was another landmark – one more harsh and frightening experience. Even loving her son had become painful.

And now here she was, putting one foot in front of the other with a hollow look in her eyes, and the only positive feelings she had were evoked by imagining a different life from the one she was living.

Yet, in the midst of all that weight, she had latched onto a universal dream. She knew something within her was crying out for something more. Yet that thing, whatever it was, seemed out of reach. No wonder life looked better in front of her than it did behind her. She ached for freedom.

Don't we all?

CHAPTER 1

THE PARABLE OF THE ACROBAT

"… you know something. What you know you can't explain, but you feel it. You've felt it your entire life, that there's something wrong with the world. You don't know what it is, but it's there, like a splinter in your mind, driving you mad."

— Morpheus, *The Matrix*

"We were meant to live for so much more, have we lost ourselves …"

— Switchfoot, *Meant to Live*

It was more than she could bear.

Life had never been particularly easy for the traveling acrobatic troupe, but this was a tragedy greater than her heart could stand. Her only child had vanished in one horrible moment. The loss was not hers alone, though. The baby boy was the smallest member of the troupe, yet he embodied their greatest hopes for the future. While his mother wept, the rest of the group continued their desperate search. Despite all their strength and skill they could not bring him back.

In the past, conversations about her son had always been charged with excitement and expectation. Today, the conversations were quiet and overshadowed by fear. The heartache of a mother for her missing child, lost in the middle of a foreign wilderness, was inconsolable. Each thought tormented her mind with dreadful possibilities. To escape the crushing weight of grief, her thoughts retreated to a safer place. Her memory replayed the joyful day, several months ago, when her son was born.

She had always been the rising star among the women of the troupe. For years they had all realized that her athletic gifts were superior to their own. She carried herself with grace and humility, yet, no other female acrobat could match her strength, agility and balance. When it was her turn to perform, even her very talented peers were mesmerized by her unique ability. They also had high regard for the man she married. He was the only other acrobat who performed with equal strength and skill. The entire troupe, already known for near superhuman feats, recognized these two as the greatest athletes they had ever seen. The couple was also well-matched as soul-mates. Instead of falling prey to inflated egos, they both possessed a gentleness of spirit and depth of character. They were dearly loved and admired, and they were the heart and soul of their community.

"He already possessed the genetic blueprint for every innate drive and ability carried by his two parents. Surely, the hope for their future was embodied in this new little creation."

When the celebrated couple announced the joyful news that they were expecting a baby, there was a great deal of excited speculation among their friends about the promising future of their child. Needless to say, everyone had high expectations for the offspring of such gifted parents. When the mother-to-be would comment on the movement of the baby inside her womb, it was met with humorous replies that, no doubt, the child was already perfecting his skills before making his debut.

On the day of his birth, the entire troupe gathered around outside in hushed anticipation, awaiting the first sound of the baby's appearance. Before he had even arrived, they all knew that he was destined to be a great acrobat. Each person carried in their own imagination the heights he would reach and the amazing feats he would perform. He already possessed the genetic blueprint for every innate drive and ability carried by his two parents. Surely, the hope for their future was embodied in this new little creation.

But today, the unthinkable had happened. Reaching into the back of the wagon to awaken her infant, she found an empty pallet. Everything else was intact, but the baby boy was nowhere to be found. Somewhere along the way he had fallen! Though they spent the day backtracking and searching for clues, the heavily traveled trails held no evidence of the tragedy. As the daylight faded, so did their hopes of ever recovering the child of promise. The somber whispers of the troupe and the sobs of his mother as she clutched the empty blankets left behind were the only evidence that the infant had even been among them. He was gone.

Rescued—or Was He?

It had to be divine intervention that protected the child from the elements and the wild animals. Sadly, his parents did not have this knowledge to reassure them. They could not have known that hours earlier that day, another man and wife made their way down the same trail. As they walked toward their modest farmland, the woman heard a sound in the brush. The sound was unusual, so they turned aside to see what it might be. Parting the grass which grew tall beside the trail, the woman looked down. Outwardly, she was shocked, but inside, a strange hope awakened as she recognized that what they had heard was a little baby, crying there in the ditch by the road.

She had agonized for much of her life over her own barrenness. Her dreams of motherhood had long ago expired. It had been years since she had allowed herself the luxury of yearning for a child to call their own. Her husband, a hard man, had long ago stopped accommodating her sadness. As a result, she bore it with quiet stoicism.

But the reality of what they had just discovered sent those once-familiar emotions cascading through her again. What was a baby doing here? The only people nearby were the neighboring farmers, tucked into the privacy of their homesteads. None of them would have brought such a young child out on this road. What should they do? Finding the child's parents might prove impossible, and if they did find them, what if they had abandoned him on purpose? If they didn't find them, what could they do? They were ill-prepared to raise a child, but they couldn't just leave him here!

She glanced at her husband, fearful of the look she might see on his face. He showed no outward reaction, but his eyes were locked on the infant. His lack of expression was familiar. The only emotion she had seen from him in recent years was anger. Times had been difficult on the farm and he had become increasingly hard. Though he was a good man, he had grown increasingly introverted, so his responses to his wife were limited, without much warmth and affection. She knew that his comfort level in raising a child would be even less than hers. He had seemed relieved when she gave up on the idea of having a baby. He could maintain their property and provide a good crop each year, but none of these things required his heart, merely his labor.

After a terse exchange, they agreed to take the child home and do all they could to find his parents or a suitable home for him. Fear gripped her. Despite her desire to be a mother, she knew she lacked the knowledge and experience to raise a child and that they had very little to offer this one. She realized that life could be very different for them, following this chance discovery, but it was impossible for her to know all that lay ahead.

She took the infant home with great trepidation. Her innate insecurity intensified at the thought of becoming a parent. Doing the best she could, she worked on the immediate task of feeding the child and finding appropriate bedding for one so small. Each cough and gurgle from the infant solicited a growing motherly affection within her, but also provoked more worry.

They knew very little about the baby they had rescued, but neither of them could have dreamed that they were holding the child of perhaps the two greatest acrobats in the world. Not only did he prove to be quite healthy, but from the very start he had a burning desire to defy gravity and to push the edge of physical limitations. He was made for more than crawling and walking—he wanted to fly. He was born for a life of transcendence.

Safe, but not Saved

As he began to grow, his natural attraction to risk and adventure would push the woman, who had been forced into motherhood, to her limits. From his first steps (which seemed premature to her) her anxiety increased daily. It seemed to her that the words coming out of her mouth the most often were "no" and "don't do that!" At first, it seemed she could not change his ways, but over time, her oppressive fear and strident objections began to take their toll. The boy was torn between the sheer joy of climbing the furniture, on one hand, and his growing love for his anxious mother on the other. His eyes would twinkle one moment and then dim the next as he gave in to her insistent protests.

The inborn desire to climb, to jump and to reach higher eventually began to waiver under the constant weight of this woman's insecurities. He did not want to disappoint or hurt her. He realized that as he pursued his own passion for adventure, it fueled the fear within her heart. To appease her, he must deny this innate drive within himself. The battle went on for years between the two of them, and it also raged within his soul. His mother observed that he was not quite himself when he stayed on the ground, but nevertheless, she felt comforted when he was not taking risks. She was certain her protective boundaries were for his own good. As he learned the importance of keeping her reassured, he learned to stifle his appetite for climbing and leaping. Disappointment moved into his little soul before he knew what to call it.

Eventually, he taught himself to be content with toys on the floor, since his mother felt more at ease when he was on the ground. However, like any mischievous child, he knew he could still feed his appetite for thrills without frightening his mother, as long as he seized opportunities when she was out of sight. On one such occasion, he climbed to the top of the icebox and precariously perched there. What a glorious view! He could see all the way into the other room. He was marveling at his new vantage point when the man and his wife walked in. The child immediately saw the panic in her eyes and knew he had hurt her. She called out to him, her voice shrill with fear and anger.

"He became skilled at working the dirt. The trees and hills no longer stirred his appetite for adventure … As his body began to change, he took on the same hard edge as his mentor."

When the man saw his wife's panic, he quickly reacted. He snatched the boy from his high perch and began to spank him. The child was aware that he had caused their fear and anger. The physical pain of the spanking, combined with the emotional pain and shame of causing all this commotion, drove home the message in an indelible way: never again would he do this to them. It was not worth the cost. The desires in his heart must die. From that day forward, he vowed that he would only look but no longer act. Whenever he stole a glance at what he was missing, the rush of adrenaline he felt only served to frustrate him further. Now even the desire itself was tied to the embarrassment and shame of having hurt his parents. *He decided that being himself was too costly.*

Life on the Farm

As days accumulated into years, the man began to take the boy out into the fields with him. A whole new panorama of adventure enticed him at the edges of the farmland. Towering trees and distant hills goaded him with heights he had never attained (and could now only dream of) and so his yearnings distracted him. As the farmer taught him the ways of cultivating the earth, the boy knew he could earn the man's respect by listening and applying his strength to hard work. He became skilled at working the dirt. The trees and hills no longer stirred his appetite for adventure. They were merely an unwelcome distraction from the farmland—the arena where he could show his true worth.

Occasionally, the farmer would catch his trainee looking up. The man's sharp words brought the youth's attention back to the task at hand. The boy could tell when the man approved of him and when he did not, and he felt keenly responsible for the man's moods. After a day of hard work, the farmer spoke almost kindly to him. On the days when the boy's suppressed yearning came to the surface, the man seemed to hold him in disdain. Therefore, he quickly learned to focus on the ground in front of him.

As his body began to change, he took on the same hard edge as his mentor, and he too became consumed with work. The man was impressed with the boy's strength and he often told him so. In years past, the deep yearnings had been a distraction; now they were not even a memory. He no longer glanced at the hills and trees. He had successfully packed away those feelings like an old set of tools—no longer useful, no longer used. They had been replaced with a new set of priorities and skills that earned him the farmer's approval and he had grown confident in their use.

He settled into the seasonal routine of the farm and he never considered any future other than the kind he saw played out in front of him each day. He was sure he was destined to work the ground—earthbound—like this farmer. However, the flickering fire of his true nature had not been entirely extinguished. The desire for adrenaline, the appetite for adventure, the need to test the strength of his body—all those things still burned deep inside of him. He didn't realize those desires were connected to his true self—the person he was meant to be. He just sensed a deep frustration from a drive he didn't know how to satisfy. Every day he see-sawed between the undefined frustration and the unsatisfied desire. When he would suppress one, the other would rise.

On certain evenings, when his work was finished, he would slip out to meet the local young men and women from the neighboring farms and they would gather together in the fields or the woods. He soon developed a reputation as an angry young man with a penchant for fighting. The pent-up strength in his muscles screamed for an outlet. It took very little provocation to unleash the volcano of his anger and frustration upon some unfortunate local farmer's son. But after a fight, he never felt relieved, just ashamed. The shame caused him to avoid his peers and he became increasingly isolated. The isolation led to more frustration and it became an endless cycle.

In the midst of this numbing routine, it seemed to be only a minor frustration when he twisted his leg one day. Once the pain had subsided, the injury left him with a limp, but it was only a small distraction in his daily work, and no hindrance in his occasional fights. He could still guide the oxen and carry heavy weights. The irregularity of his limp was just one more thing to endure in his life on the farm. The years passed and the routine of the farm soaked into him like the rays of the sun, season after season. The farmer and his wife endured parenthood with the same stoic resignation they relied on whilst waiting out the next dry season. Welcome or not, it was the hand life had dealt them.

The Familiarity of the Unfamiliar

One day something happened to interrupt his familiar routine. Like so many life-changing events, it was unexpected, almost an intrusion. He saw a poster at the general store and was intrigued. The feelings it evoked were subliminal, but interest in the event would not leave his mind and he felt uneasy and distracted from his work. The poster displayed all kinds of apparatus that could be used to defy gravity. He saw a swing that looked like a bar suspended above the ground, a wire stretched across an expanse with people walking on it, and many other strangely shaped contraptions. Every one of them seemed designed to be climbed or to help one become airborne.

The pictures seemed to grow in his mind, both in size and intensity, until they swirled around somewhere inside him. His interest turned to fascination and his fascination produced invasive images that unnerved him. They were like memories, but no thought accompanied them. Like a word almost remembered, on the tip of the tongue, sensation haunted him. Something about this poster captured him and wouldn't let go. The acrobats were coming to town!

The campaign to go to the show was relatively easy and ultimately successful. After only a few objections, the man and his wife gave in and the plans were made. The timing of the show actually allowed all of them to attend, so they planned to make a day of it. Chores around the farm were rearranged so they could take a day off and all that remained was waiting.

As the day drew nearer, he became more unsettled. What was this gnawing sensation he had? Why would he be nervous? It was not he who was performing. However, the night before the show he dreamed that he *was* the one performing. He could see the ground far below him as he hurtled through the air on the trapeze. He felt free—like a child—in his dream. As he awoke, his familiar surroundings felt more like a dream and his dream seemed more like the reality of being awake.

"He was so energized by what he was feeling, he never suspected that the entire course of his life was about to change."

On the day of the show he awoke early and the day could not pass quickly enough. He had enough work to keep him busy for the day, but he found it very difficult to think about farming. Despite the years of careful training, his mind would not stay focused on the fields. Instead, his imagination replayed last night's dream and his emotions relived the feeling he had as he swung through the air.

It was finally time to go and he hurried his parents across the city streets to the tent set up on the edge of town. As they entered with the crowds he felt overtaken by the atmosphere. All kinds of strange apparatus were spread around the ground and suspended from the top of the tent. Each one seemed to glisten with possibility. They all implied the promise of freeing the earthbound from the constraints of gravity. The young man felt as though his insides would crawl right out of his skin. The gnawing sensation he had carried for days now changed to excitement.

Then the moment came when the troupe of acrobats entered the tent and began their performance. He was so engrossed that he could scarcely breathe. He was motionless as every fiber of his being connected with what he was witnessing. His muscles twitched, his heart jumped, and he could feel the rush of air, though he remained in his seat. He was outside of himself watching these amazing men and women. He felt air filling his lungs and life pulsing through him in a way that should have been familiar.

All too soon the show was over. All around the tent acrobats took time to mingle with the audience. They signed posters, did minor demonstrations of strength and agility, and talked with the people who had come to see them. The young man could not take it in fast enough. He went from apparatus to apparatus asking questions and talking to the various performers. In the midst of all his excitement, he lost track of the man and woman who had raised him. He was so energized by what he was feeling, he never suspected that the entire course of his life was about to change.

The Discovery

The farmer and his wife had been standing by, silently waiting for the young man to complete his tour. They were vaguely aware that a pair of older acrobats stood within several feet of them, not as eager to engage the curious fans. The woman had the look of one who had suffered much in life, while her husband seemed to be kind and protective of her. A few words were exchanged, opening conversation between the two couples. They were close enough in age so that small talk was comfortable. As they exchanged pleasantries, the female acrobat noticed the woman's constant surveillance of the young man.

"Is he yours?" she inquired.

The hesitation on the faces of the farming couple was noticeable, before they nodded back.

"You have kept a careful eye on him," the acrobat said. "I notice he doesn't get far out of your sight."

"You know how mothers worry," the farmer said to the couple. "She always knows where he is."

The acrobat's eyes went to the ground and she seemed to wince. She spoke softly, "A mother *should* worry ... her child is a precious possession."

"You have children?" asked the farmer's wife.

"We did ... once," the man replied, knowing his wife still could not talk about this subject easily.

"I'm sorry," said the farmer's wife. "What happened?"

The man began telling the story of their baby's disappearance, to spare his wife the difficulty. He shared their painful experience, beginning with their great joy at the birth of their son and recounting his disappearance from the wagon train. He even described the agonizing details of their subsequent fruitless search. At the end of the story, he told them that they believed their son had been lost not far from this very town.

The farmer and his wife were first stunned, then horrified. They knew the implication of what it meant to them, personally. They recognized the details—the year, the month, and the location where they had found the baby. They stood, open-mouthed, listening to the acrobats tell their story. It was obvious that time had not diminished the pain of their loss. When they had finished, the farmer and his wife looked pale and overwhelmed, not knowing how to respond. The woman was shaking and her husband was holding her tightly around the shoulders, as if to keep her from sinking to the ground. For the first time, the acrobats took notice of how this couple was receiving their tale, and they were surprised by the reaction. The farmer's wife kept looking back and forth from the acrobats to the boy. Tears welled up in her eyes, and fear and joy enveloped her at the same time. Finally she spoke.

"The boy does not belong to us … he belongs to you," she stuttered.

"What's that?" asked the acrobats, still not realizing what she was trying to say.

"The boy … we found him on the side of the road … there was nothing to identify him …". Then the farmer's wife blurted out the rest of the revelation: "So we took him home!"

Now it was the acrobats' turn to be stunned. At first, they couldn't grasp it all at once, but then the realization hit them like a tidal wave. Through questions and tears they tried to embrace the truth, but it was too big, it was too much! For a moment, it looked like the woman might faint. Now it was her turn to gaze at the young man and then back at the farming couple. She fought back tears of joy as she was enveloped in the long-forgotten feeling of hope.

When the truth finally connected, the acrobat's wife began to move toward the young man on the other side of the tent. Her husband restrained her from the impulse to rush toward her son to reclaim him as her own. It was clear to him that the other couple had acted benevolently to save their child's life, and that these adoptive parents were the only family their son could remember. What was not clear was what they should do next. Both couples stared at each other.

The young man had finished his conversation and was approaching the four adults. Immediately he sensed the maelstrom of emotion. He wasn't surprised to see the unsteady look on the face of the woman who had raised him, but he was very puzzled at the odd expression on the farmer's face.

"What is it?" he asked, puzzled. "Is everything all right?"

"As the young man paused to take it all in, he was struck by another thought: he had a choice to make ... He had to choose between the familiar reality his mind knew and the unknown truth that resonated in his heart."

The silence that followed was so heavy that he felt suffocated. He looked at the two people he had lived and worked with all of his life. Then he looked at the handsome strangers who stood next to them. All four studied his face intently, each one wanting to hug him, but none knowing if they should.

"Is everything all right?" he asked again.

The sudden torrent of their words washed over him. Both women tried to speak their hearts, simultaneously. In the confusion, the farmer stepped forward and put a hand on the young man's shoulder. The others grew silent.

"Son," he said (he had never called him son before now). "Son, I know you have been with us on the farm as long as you can remember, but it is time that you knew something."

The woman who was a stranger stepped close to him and put her hand on his shoulder. She was gazing at him with tears in her eyes and he thought it was odd that she seemed unable to take her hand off his shoulder, since he didn't even know her. Even more foreign to him was the emotion in the voice of the man he had known all these years. He had never heard him express himself this way before. He knew something life-changing was happening.

THE CHOICE

"Son, we are not who you *think* we are," the farmer said, his voice quivering, "and because of that *you* are not who you think you are."

As the man tried to gently explain, the acrobat's husband edged closer. The farmer's wife also was drawing near. As they all shared the story about his origins—filling in the blanks in his own memory—his confusion turned into questions, and his unbelief gave way to the swelling truth. Now it was his turn to look intently between the two couples. He looked first at the farmer and his wife, then at the strangers who had given him life. The battle inside raged like never before. His thoughts bombarded him and his emotions swirled around as he tried to understand and absorb the rapid-fire story. Some things suddenly made sense and yet nothing made sense. In fact, it might take years for his thoughts to catch up to what was happening to him on this day.

As the young man paused to take it all in, he was struck by another thought: *he had a choice to make.* He looked to his left where the farmer stood, looking worn, and his adoptive mother gazed back at him tearfully. They were his family (or were they?). Their home was all he had ever known. Their voices and their ways were so familiar to him. Yet, at that moment, he saw them differently than before.

Standing at his right were these two strangers (or were they?) who had known him at the beginning and had hoped and searched for him all his life. They were not merely *different* from him, they seemed superhuman! Yet, they claimed that their blood ran through his veins. Just by their existence they declared him to be more than he dared to dream, and he had a choice to make.

The farmer studied his wife's face, and then spoke aloud what they were all thinking. His voice was unsteady, but he said, "Son, you know we could never prevent you from joining your true family, now that you know."

The moment was thick. Silence hung over the group like a brewing storm. A small crowd had gathered. The acrobats and locals alike began to realize what was happening and whisper to one another. The young man looked back and forth between the two couples who represented two very different cultures. All four looked at him with a strange mixture of hope and fear. Emotions pulsed in his throat. The choice was his and the others knew the weight of it.

He looked at the farmer and his wife. All that was familiar was connected to those two people. To leave them behind was unthinkable, after all they had given him. Though he was afraid to leave them, it was more than that: he had no picture of any other kind of life. The memory of his past was rooted in the farm, and those experiences shaped his expectations for the future. He *felt* like a farmer, he *thought* like a farmer; he even saw the world through the eyes of a farmer. Could it be possible that he truly was not a farmer?

When he looked at the acrobats he believed what they had told him, but he had difficulty connecting to it. Life with them would be foreign and unimaginable. The searing in his chest told him he belonged with them; he felt powerfully drawn to them, yet his mind drew back. He had always hungered for what he now could not comprehend. He had to choose between the familiar reality his mind knew and the unknown truth that resonated in his heart.

The adults also recognized the struggle he was going through. The farmer and his wife knew they never could have prepared him for the life he was born to live. Their own fear of losing him was compounded by the realization that, even if he stayed, he could never be the same. The acrobats wanted to convince him to come with them, but they knew he would be starting from square one, so he must decide for himself. His mother wanted to grab him and never let go. His father was overcome with joy, but also knew that his son was not prepared to make such an important choice ... how could he be? He had no idea about the life of an acrobat, traveling from place to place.

Finally, the young man spoke. Choked with emotion and still torn, he first turned to address the couple who raised him: "Mom and Dad," he said lovingly, "I have known you all my life. The life you showed me is all I have ever seen, though part of me has always wondered if there was something more that I was missing."

Then he turned to his birth parents and continued, "And the life you are telling me is mine, I can only dream of. Strangely, I *have* dreamed of it, and I am not sure I could go through life without experiencing what I cannot even imagine right now. In one way, your life is completely foreign to me, yet you tell me that it is the life I was meant to live. What seems like a choice really is no choice at all. If I do not go

"The drive for freedom is like our appetite like hunger, unconscious and automatic, like blinking your eyes when something strikes out at you."

with you, I will continue to live a familiar life that was never meant for me. My mind is made up. I will simply have to let the rest of me catch up." He slowly turned back to the farmer and his wife. "I must go with these acrobats and become who I really am."

It was a profound moment. Large as it was, it still seemed to all five of them that something more important than they could know had happened to them. That day, circumstances changed and could never be the same. Even the onlookers realized that none of them could ever view the world or themselves the same way again.

> "He came to His own and those who were his own did not receive Him. But as many as received Him, to them He gave the right to become children of God, even to those who believe in His name, who were born not of blood, nor of the will of man, but of God." (John 1:11-13)

> "Beloved, now we are children of God, and it has not appeared as yet what we shall be. We know that when He appears, we shall be like Him, because we will see Him just as He is." —John the Apostle writing about Jesus (1 John 3:2)

CHAPTER 2
FREEDOM AND BONDAGE

"None are so hopelessly enslaved as those who falsely believe they are free."

— Goethe

"I still haven't found what I'm looking for."

— Bono, U2

FReeDOM.

Wars have been fought over it. Nations have been birthed and destroyed in the name of it. Siblings fight over it. Parents argue with adolescents to define it. Life, freedom and the pursuit of happiness: these three things are intertwined with one another. They are so hard-wired into us that they drive us to action and, in some cases, destruction – the destruction of the very freedom we are pursuing. The drive for freedom is like our appetite like hunger, unconscious and automatic, like blinking your eyes when something strikes out at you. Even our drive for self-preservation is rooted in our instinct to lunge toward freedom.

We each have a variety of appetites. The one common to all of us is the appetite for food. At times, my desire for a cheeseburger has compelled me to walk, drive and overcome all sorts of obstacles in order to satisfy that craving. It's strange how hunger will invade and even shape my thoughts. Sometimes the project in front of me begins to remind me of French fries. Appetites will do that. We also have an appetite for freedom. In fact, it is part of what makes us human. Most of us do not realize how constantly, nor how strongly, this appetite compels us. When the urge for freedom arises, we tend to look for an escape route from our frustrations. When we get the chance to go out or get away for the weekend, it feels as if our prison door is opening.

This is a normal craving for freedom that we all experience from time to time – the freedom to break from the monotony of routine and do something a little more adventurous for a while. But there are much more extreme cases. There are those who, feeling trapped in a never ending downward spiral, scream out for freedom. They seek relief from the battle they have been fighting. They may even have given up on life because they are so blinded by their own hopelessness and frustration to see any other way out. This book has been written to help all who pursue freedom to find it, whatever their circumstances.

> *"People will labor and fight for whatever they consider to be freedom."*

After my years working in the juvenile system, I went back to school and opened up a counseling practice. For fifteen years I sat across from wives, mothers, husbands, fathers – one after another – each of them in some way echoing the woman whose story I told in the prologue, all searching for freedom. During that phase of my life, I saw and spoke with that specific woman again, and I believe she moved much closer to *real* freedom.

Working as a counselor, I watched all types of people work overtime to satisfy the impulse for freedom. In fact, the only reason I had met them at all was because they had defined freedom in such a way that their pursuit of it had backfired. After seeing so many good people fight a good fight and then fall, I have begun to learn what real freedom is and (just as important) what it is not. People will labor and fight for whatever they consider to be freedom. Those who contend for accurate and true definitions find not only freedom, but peace. Those who pursue an incomplete or misguided definition will fight a sincere (but often exhausting) fight, and then they find themselves in a condition worse than when they began. The book you

We must define "freedom" accurately

hold in your hands was birthed through fifteen years of untangling relational knots and fighting for the freedom of individuals and families. Through those years of counseling, I learned how to ask the right kind of questions. If you ask the wrong question, no answer will satisfy – even the right answer to that question. So before we talk about how to find freedom, we need to define it. Perhaps the best way to define freedom is to understand its opposite: *bondage*.

Bondage

Stuck ... blocked ... trapped ... frustrated ... dissatisfied – these are the words people use to describe life when they are, indeed, stuck. What they are referring to is, in fact, *bondage*. It manifests itself in two main forms: either a deep dissatisfaction that never seems to go away, or an enslavement to destructive habits or other negative patterns of living that we can't break free from. The two are connected; these destructive habits and patterns arise out of our misguided attempts to quench our dissatisfaction. When someone is not at liberty to live life as they want to or when certain factors are hindering their progress, they are in bondage.

If a simple definition of the first type of bondage is "the condition of the dissatisfied", then the majority of us suffer from some degree of bondage in our lives. Generally, we are a dissatisfied people. We need more money, more time, and more of what someone else seems to have. We think that if we had what they have, life would finally work for us. This type of bondage is the seemingly unquenchable search for satisfaction so eloquently described for us by the Rolling Stones when they sang, "I Can't Get No Satisfaction." In fact, the lyric expresses this peculiar irony: the more desperately we seek satisfaction, the further away it seems to be and the less of it we seem to find. How odd when, in contrast, one of the great proponents of freedom in all of history, Jesus of Nazareth, declared, "Ask, and it will be given to you; seek, and you will find…" So was He just making that stuff up? Does it really work that way? And if it works for everybody else, why doesn't it work that way for me? "Cuz I've tried and I've tried," as Mick Jagger said.

For the majority of us, however, the outward frustrations we experience aren't as common or as relentless as the ones coming from within. This is the second type of bondage – <u>the inexorable draw of our own bad habits</u>, ranging from the innocuous to the dangerous. How many times have we heard people say, "I'll start that new eating plan tomorrow ... This is a really bad time for me to quit smoking – I'm under so much stress right now ... I know I shouldn't go further in debt to buy this, but it might not be on sale when I can finally pay cash." We try to convince ourselves that eventually we will "grow out" of our habit, or we will work on it at a more convenient time, or hope that it might simply go away. Yet we find the same old problems cropping up time and again.

"If we possess the ability to look honestly and objectively at our life, then we will realize how stuck we are and want to do something about it ... The problem is, often our solutions are as bad or worse than the problem we began with."

What about our endless struggle with the same old character flaws that keep hindering our progress toward freedom at every turn? We find excuses for our shortcomings or, worse, blame them on others: "I know I shouldn't get so angry and lose my temper, but he/she just has a way of pushing my buttons ... It seems like every job I get, I always get assigned to a supervisor that just doesn't understand me or the way I work." In those moments we have a rising awareness that things are not as they should be. <u>We think that life seems to be working for others</u> but not for us. My neighbor seems to be happy. My co-workers don't seem to face these frustrations. Fed up with the road we've traveled in life, we set out to change our course; we turn left this time, instead of right – only to discover that we end up back where we started ... still stuck ... and with more time lost.

TRYING TO BREAK THE CYCLE

If we possess the ability to look honestly and objectively at our life, then we will realize how stuck we are and want to do something about it.

Recognizing their lack of freedom, people will torture themselves with questions such as, "What *is* freedom? Can I really attain it? Can I really be free in my set of circumstances? What if I always have these circumstances?" Those kinds of questions will keep driving people forward in a quest for freedom or they will end up driving people crazy. Such questions reveal and describe the experience of being in bondage: stuck and getting stucker. Maybe the constant questioning is just as much a part of the trap.

Others who fail to be as honest with themselves are in denial. A very common trap is to avoid even acknowledging that we are stuck. Yet, whether we choose to face it or not, eventually our condition will demand our attention. It usually happens this way: walking through life, we encounter frustrations. Some of these are ongoing, minor frustrations – like cars cutting us off on the road or, worse, a series of painful, frustrating relationships. Others are major frustrations: our marriage ends; our dreams seem to die in front of us as we lose a child; our possessions are destroyed in a natural disaster; or we lose our money through economic crisis or, even worse, someone else takes it from us.

When such frustrations come, we want to take action; we want to come up with a solution that will take away the frustration and release us. The problem is, often our solutions are as bad or worse than the problem we began with.

Maybe we change our career path to pursue a larger salary. Maybe we compromise a value because it doesn't seem to be paying off. Perhaps we even decide to scrap it all and start over with a new family, a new town or job. We change our circumstances hoping for relief, and relief comes temporarily, as it did to the young car thief's mother in the prologue who drove out of state. Old things are behind us, and the slate in front of us appears clean and waiting for a new beginning. We must finally be free!

But then it happens again. The pattern repeats. The frustrations rise. The circumstances start to close in. The new family seems like the old family, only now we are contending with both of them. The new relationship seems a lot like the old one, but certain ties with the old one can never be completely severed, so the wound takes much longer to heal than we planned. We never quite obtain what we had hoped: a fresh, clean slate to begin anew. After a while, we realize that instead of things getting better, it seems they have gotten more complicated. That habit we thought we had conquered shows up again in a different form.

At this point, we begin to consider that maybe, just maybe, we are completely stuck. We either repeat the cycle, look for relief again, or we begin to swallow hard and resign ourselves to the hopelessness of our life. These bills will never be paid. My relationships will never be satisfying. I am bound for unhappiness or disappointment. With soul-numbing resignation, we pull up the covers of our life, assuming this is the bed in which we must lie.

Sometimes the more energetic people – the more driven ones – simply smile and try to convince everyone else that they are okay. Outwardly they project "Life is working for me!" yet inwardly they are thinking, "I would hate anyone to know that I am secretly dissatisfied." Some people's solution is to "fake it till they make it". Hoping to fool themselves and others, they bury a growing sense of emptiness underneath a complex set of defenses. They accumulate possessions, accolades and skills (or just toys) to hide from their own dissatisfaction and convince themselves and others, "I have discovered the secret."

We pursue what looks like freedom. We either escalate our pursuit (feeling certain that just around the next turn is the life we've been looking for) or we finally begin to give up. Buried by the mounting evidence that change and freedom are myths, we loosen our grip, lower our expectations and settle: "I will never lose that extra weight ... I will always struggle with anger ... Face it, I'm never going to write that book ..." and the list goes on.

WHICH IS WORSE, THE PROBLEM OR THE SOLUTION?

Our appetite for freedom motivates our momentary responses, but it also shapes a lifelong quest. It is so deep in us that it often pushes us before we even realize it. When this appetite drives us, the very actions we take to obtain freedom can actually push real freedom out of reach. It is like a child learning to use his hands for the first time. He reaches for his pacifier but, instead, pushes it off the high chair. It is a common experience for many that despite how fervently they pursue their dreams, the life they are reaching for moves further away, instead of closer.

One of the most consistent lessons I learned in my counseling practice was that, in many cases, the "solutions" people apply to their lives can create greater obstacles to freedom than their problems. In other words, they begin with a problem and set out to apply a solution, but this solution, inaccurately conceived and fervently applied, eventually leads them to seek more counseling than the original problem would have required. Let me illustrate.

When I was sixteen, I received a call for help from my aunt. Her car had a flat tire on a cold winter day. I jumped in my parents' car and went to help her. The flat tire was the problem. I was supposed to be the solution, so I began to equip myself to solve her simple problem. Reaching into the trunk of her car, I discovered a secondary problem: she had no lug wrench. Now remember, I was sixteen, therefore, I did not recognize the lack of the lug wrench as a significant problem for me. I found a perfectly functioning lug wrench in the back of my parents' Volkswagen and I walked over to my aunt's Chevy and went to work. I quickly discovered what some might have considered another problem: my German lug wrench was just a fraction too big for my aunt's American lug-nuts. Again, being a sixteen-year-old male – not a problem! I simply decided to use the tools at hand and try again. It was no time at all before the massive strength of my sixteen-year-old muscles had stripped those lug nuts of any meaningful shape. I whittled them down to smooth round protrusions, unable to be gripped by any lug wrench at all, much less the ill-fitted one in my hand.

"If you've been working really hard and the problem is getting worse, not better, then consider the possibility that you have been using the wrong tools."

My faulty solution left us in a far worse condition than the original problem. At this point, we had to call in professionals with power tools and have the car towed. Notice, the solution did not fail for lack of effort or even for lack of forcefulness; the solution failed because of the forceful, fervent application of the wrong tool. If you've been working really hard

Great insight

and the problem is getting worse, not better, then consider the possibility that you have been using the wrong tools. The good news is that the same effort, using the right tools, can change everything.

Time and again in my counseling practice, I witnessed this very dynamic at work. Good people with character and diligence found themselves stuck; and the harder they tried to solve their problems, the worse their circumstances seemed to become. In addition, the worse the situation became, the harder they tried, and I saw them sink into a downward spiral of frustration and hopelessness. Oftentimes, our faulty solutions create a whole new category of problems. We must find a real way out of this mess. We must find the proper tools.

If we can accurately define the problem first, then we can better identify what tools we need. The size of the lug-nuts on the car dictated the size of the lug-wrench required to solve the problem. We must examine the problem at hand to determine what tools are needed to obtain true and lasting freedom.

THREE LEVELS OF BONDAGE

One of the first keys to unlocking our situation and finding freedom is to understand the nature of bondage, how we get into it and, more importantly, how we can get out of it. If I could state it simply, there are three levels of bondage that must be negotiated in sequence in order to find true freedom:

1) bondage to **bad definitions**
2) bondage to **ourselves**
3) bondage to a variety of **obstacles**

Look at how these three aspects of bondage operate in the following example:

I was driving behind a lady on a four-lane road many years ago. She was in the far right lane and I was directly behind her. She then decided that she wanted to move one lane to the left, so she switched on her left-turn signal and slowed down. What happened next? Everyone behind her (and behind me) began to move left, in order to pass her car and, as a result, a continuous line of cars formed in the lane where she wanted to be. She could not merge to that lane because of the passing cars, so she continued to slow down, her signal light still flashing, and more and more cars continued to pass her. The harder she tried, the more she was stuck.

The very thing she was doing to reach her goal was the very thing pushing her goal out of reach. She had a clear picture of what she wanted, but the method she chose actually built a wall between where she was and where she wanted to be. Imagine then, her frustration as she finally arrived in the left lane, only to realize that she needed to exit the freeway soon afterwards, but couldn't do so from the new lane she occupied. After all that work, she needed to get back in the far-right lane to exit. She had incorrectly assessed the situation and therefore had prevented her own freedom from the freeway.

This driver has given us a clear picture of the three levels of bondage in operation. In order to get free she needed to know:

1. Which lane she needed to be in and why – *to have an accurate definition of her situation.*
2. How she was preventing her own progress – *to recognize the way in which she was keeping herself "stuck".*
3. How to get into the lane she desired – *to understand what obstacles blocked her from her destination and how to negotiate them.*

Her first problem was that she had defined her goal as "getting to the other lane". She was unaware that her desired exit was only a little further up the road in her current lane. This wrong definition of her situation marshaled her efforts in the wrong direction. A bad definition of our target will always guide our best efforts in the wrong direction. Good answers to bad questions are still not "good" answers. People must first get free from *bad definitions* because we will instinctively lunge toward anything we consider to be freedom. If our definition is inaccurate in any way, then the instinct for freedom will backfire on us, driving our goal further out of reach.

Her second problem was that she was hindering her own progress. She employed a faulty strategy in order to get where she wanted to be. Her own maneuvering contributed to creating an impassable line of cars. Had she been able to look at the situation objectively – from anywhere other than her own car – then she could have easily seen the nature of her predicament. Her bad definition combined with her own limited point of view led her to a solution that made her problem worse, not better. She slowed down and put on her turn signal and then she became her own obstacle. Once our definitions have some clarity to them we must then get free from ourselves. Armed with an accurate definition of our situation, we generally find that "being ourselves" is actually part of the problem. Not understanding who we are is the reason that many of us have an inaccurate definition of freedom. Without this vital knowledge about our identity, all other attempts to gain freedom launch us on a journey without an actual destination.

The third problem the driver in our example faced was some real obstacles. A stream of cars now blocked her passage into the next lane. Even if she now recognized her own role in creating the trap, she still had to negotiate these obstacles to achieve her goal and there was no guarantee that they would automatically move out of her way.

Getting free from bondage we face a similar challenge. Even if we have both an accurate definition and recognize our role in hindering our own progress, we still need to work on those things that many people try to tackle first: *life obstacles.* Can you see the dilemma here? People consistently try to deal with the obstacles in their life first, without either a proper definition of their situation or any real understanding of their identity. Then they labor for a lifetime wondering why things are getting steadily worse and not better.

> *"People consistently try to deal with the obstacles in their life first, without either a proper definition of their situation or any real understanding of their identity."*

Apply these same levels to the acrobat from our story. Imagine if he had defined freedom as simply controlling his temper, or overcoming his frustration, but never came to know who he really was. He could have worked hard to overcome obstacles and still never found true freedom. He first had to define freedom correctly as "becoming who he was born to be". He then had to make the switch: he was an acrobat, not a farmer. Once he made the switch, he could then begin to work on any obstacles in his life. But imagine if he had simply overcome his dissatisfaction, *but continued to live as a farmer!* His solution would actually have magnified his real problem. This is why it is essential that we deal with the three levels of bondage, in order, if we are to achieve true and lasting freedom.

Over the years, I have noticed that progressing through these three levels in our journey is like unwrapping a cleverly wrapped gift: peeling off each layer gets us one step closer to the gift inside. We must make some headway on the first layer before we can even see, or deal with, the next one. Unlike progressing through levels on a career path, these three levels are more similar to the stages of human development. Each level provides a foundation for the next, and understanding each level is necessary before we can successfully negotiate the next. For example: we must get into our car before we can get out of our driveway, and we must get out of our driveway before we can get on the highway.

Bad Definitions and Counterfeits of Freedom

Let's look in more detail at the three levels of bondage. First, the trap of *bad definitions*. If a person has a faulty definition of what constitutes freedom, then nothing they do will set them free, no matter how much effort they expend in the process. Remember that our need for freedom is such an intense drive that once we set our sights on something which we believe will achieve it, we will move toward it magnetically. This is why a *bad definition* is the first and greatest level of bondage – people are in bondage to their *own definition* of freedom, and an inaccurate definition that cannot produce freedom will just produce further bondage.

This explains why so many strong people are stuck in life. The stronger the person, the more they struggle, and the quicker they become entrenched. Like the opponent of a black belt in Judo, their own strength works against them. People with good intentions, strong wills, great perseverance, and unswerving diligence can wake up one day and wonder why they feel so stuck. Like the knit finger trap won at carnivals, the harder it's pulled, the more force is directed toward escaping and the more firmly the trap holds. The importance of a clear and accurate definition of freedom is that the rest of the journey depends on starting at the right place and aiming at the right target. Many counterfeits exist that look a lot like freedom at the outset, but the outcome of pursuing these decoys is further "stuckness" because they each constitute a bad definition. Here are some examples of these counterfeits to freedom.

Counterfeit #1: Freedom is the absence of boundaries

When people define freedom as the absence of boundaries, it is like an animal with no fences. The adolescent who believes his parents are holding him back fights against them in a number of ways. Every battle leads to further restriction. So until he realizes the role that his own irresponsibility and immaturity play in his frustration, he will continue to dig himself into a deeper hole. This is the common trap in adolescence, but when we don't learn the lesson there, then its subtle deception often carries over into the rest of our lives. Because boundaries are frustrating, we believe that the boundaries are the cause of the stuck-ness. It works like this: We want to do something, but we run into a wall. For example, we don't have enough money … our boss won't let us off work … our spouse resents some desire we have that is part of our true nature. The variety of "fences" is endless. The trap occurs when we believe that removing these obstacles will make us free, because then our freedom depends on someone else. We have granted them control over us. It is the belief itself that has us stuck, not the boundary.

> *"Our need for freedom is such an intense drive that once we set our sights on something which we believe will achieve it, we will move toward it magnetically."*

Counterfeit #2: Freedom is the absence of frustrating habits

This second counterfeit focuses on treating the symptoms instead of the root cause: "I drink too much, therefore, if I stop drinking, I will be free … If I stop screaming, stop pulling out my eye-lashes, stop whatever compulsive behavior seems to be the source of frustration for me and my loved ones, then and only then will I finally be free." We assume that when we are free *from* drinking, yelling, pornography, etc, then we will be free. We can imagine what a relief it will be when these things no longer control us, so we assume their departure heralds the arrival of freedom. The difficulty with this counterfeit is the human propensity to substitute one habit for another until we find real freedom. Quite often, the behaviors we want to change are outward symptoms of the freedom we *lack* inwardly. To change a behavior without experiencing true freedom leads to great frustration and, eventually, to a sense of powerlessness and even hopelessness. We had hoped to escape from a pit that now seems even deeper.

Counterfeit #3: Freedom will come when my circumstances or relationships change

The third counterfeit is a devastating decoy for freedom. Many a family has disintegrated at the hands of this deadly definition: the belief that we will be free when we get out of the circumstances or relationships that seem to bind us. Our growing dissatisfaction is often taken out on the nearest meaningful relationship, whether it be our spouse, our kids, or someone with whom we work. We think, "Surely this situation or these people are keeping me stuck." If we are struggling in our marriage, freedom must be the result of getting out of that marriage and getting into a new one, right? Nothing could be further from the truth. Yet, this is a commonly held belief and a decoy that is frequently followed into the trap.

So What Is Freedom?

I have provided an overview of some common misconceptions about freedom. If the above misconceptions are not accurate definitions of freedom, what is it then? We know that, like studying a map to accurately determine our destination, our quest for freedom must begin with an accurate definition of freedom. So what is the target we are actually shooting for? I would like to state it simply and then I'll elaborate.

> *"Freedom is the ability to act and react in life as the man or woman you were created to be."*

Don't pass this by too quickly. The sentence is short. The idea is even simple. It is the many counterfeits and decoys of freedom preoccupying us that cause us to bypass the true definition too quickly. So often, the things that prevent us from being ourselves go unrecognized. Freedom is never about our outward circumstances, it is always about becoming ourselves *within* our circumstances. The evidence of true freedom is when we can act and react without insecurity … without judgment … without fear … without rage … without selfishness … without codependency … the list goes on.

"Every human being is born with natural desires that have been 'hijacked' to destructively program our mind with this dead end, default setting. The good news is that we can actually be recreated from the inside out."

I will never forget sitting across a metal table in a locked detention area facing a young woman who was trying to scare me away. She had brutally assaulted someone, resulting in their death. She looked at me through hate-filled eyes and began to let me know why I should be afraid of her. She ended her presentation with these words: "I am the worst person you'll ever meet."

Whether out of courage or ignorance I am still not sure, but I met her gaze and responded immediately with the question, "What if you're not?"

Her resolve wavered for a moment and she said, "What do you mean?"

I responded, "What if you're *not* the worst person I'll ever meet? In fact, what if you're not really wicked *at all?*" I continued. "What if you're really just a little girl who has been through terribly painful circumstances and all you really know is what you have felt ... and what if that feeling isn't who you are at all?" Now her resolve did more than waver, she flinched. For a split second, I was sure I could see a scared little girl instead of a murderous woman. I knew I had hit a nerve.

Freedom From Yourself—or— When YOU are the Trap

Like this woman, too often we let our circumstances in life define who we are, and we grow up believing we are someone completely different than who we *really* are. A definition of freedom that does not include an understanding of our identity will always lead us astray. For this young lady, the ability to act and react to life, separately from the picture she had of herself, would make all the difference in the world. Again, freedom is the ability to act and react in life as the man or woman you were *created* to be.

The next two levels of bondage are *ourselves* and our *obstacles*. If we try to address the obstacles in our life without some idea of who we truly are, it would be like trying to take a trip without first choosing a destination – we're not going to get where we need to go. We must learn what it means to be *free from ourselves*.

Jesus of Nazareth, who seemed to know something about freedom, recognized this trap. He recognized, first and foremost, that we are not just in bondage to our misunderstandings about freedom, but we are also in bondage to being *ourselves*. His purpose on earth was to free us from the trap of being who we are. He knew that disconnection from the true Source of life is the universal problem and condition of all mankind. So Jesus came to correct our misconceptions about freedom, about God, and about ourselves; but He also came to make a way to replace our old self with a new self – to actually reconnect us to the Source of life so that we could think differently and live differently. In fact, the very thing He asked us to do – "repent" – literally means "to think differently afterwards". He knew that our flawed way of thinking (as well as our old definitions) would keep us from enjoying the very freedom He came to give us. It is important to grasp the contrast between what Jesus wants us to do and what we repeatedly try to do. He says we need to *think differently*, whereas we continually try to *think different*, i.e. to change the content of our thoughts. There is a vital difference: to think *differently* refers to the *way in which we think*; to think *different* refers to *what* we think.

Sadly, we think that when Jesus tells us to repent, He is asking us to change the content of our minds: i.e. "Stop stealing, start praying, stop cursing, start giving ..." But this is merely exchanging bad content for good content and the knowledge of evil for the knowledge of good. If we merely *think different*, then the best we can hope for is that, once again, we will try harder. But if we *think differently*, it is as if we change the lenses over our eyes and the filters over our ears. When we see things differently it becomes almost impossible to do things the same way and, therefore, real change can happen.

One time a computer programmer came into my counseling office for help. After describing the wreck he had made of his life, he summed up his condition using the terminology of his profession: "I don't just need reprogramming, I need a new motherboard!" The thing that separates us from God, commonly known as sin, is like a computer virus that so pervades our system that the central processing unit must be replaced. Our CPU, our spirit, must be made new so that we can begin to clear out the bad "files" we have stored and replace them with healthy ones that work *for* us, not *against* us.

Just like a bad default setting, our wrong thought patterns keep leading us to the same dead end targets – the same counterfeits of freedom. The reality is that every human being is born with natural desires that have been "hijacked" to destructively program our mind with this dead end, default setting. The good news is that we can actually be recreated from the inside out. We don't have to stay "stuck". We'll talk more about that later.

Our self-destructive condition is sometimes obvious, sometimes not so obvious. It might be manifesting in all sorts of external ways, but the root of the problem is internal. I'm not really telling you anything you don't already know. We all know it, we all sense that something inside is not right. For example: how comfortable are you with being alone with yourself? If you were to take away what we call "white noise" – the constant hum of distraction that is so prevalent in Western society – does the thought of being alone in absolute stillness with your conscience, your inner voice, provoke in you a certain amount of anxiety? Even as you read this, are you inclined to avoid acknowledging such a thing?

Until we recognize and get free of the *bondage of ourselves*, we will be stuck in a vicious cycle. Driven to find freedom, we pursue an escape, and the escape route leads us into the very thing that has us trapped. Then the cycle begins all over again. It is this dynamic that leads so many into deeper bondage and dissatisfaction, even though they are pursuing freedom with all their strength.

So many of the people I counseled were fighting against some external circumstance: trying to get their wife to change, to get their family to understand them, to get their boss to recognize their talent – all in the name of finally being free. This is not only the condition of many individuals, but the collective instinct of the human race and it reveals to us the fundamental trap: to one degree or another, we are all stuck being the person we have become. When we discover a pattern in our life of running from circumstances or people, we finally begin to realize that *they* were never the culprit – it was *us*. The saying is true: "Wherever you go, there you are!" Until we can honestly address the trap of our own humanity, no other obstacle can be finally and fully removed. Once we address the fact that *we are the trap*, we are free to address the third level – the one that is more evident to most of us – the bondage of *external obstacles* in our life.

STUFF GETS IN THE WAY

Legitimate obstacles to our freedom really do exist and they must be identified and dealt with. As with our first level, identifying these obstacles inaccurately causes us to stay stuck, and using the wrong tools to change them is likely to add to our stuck-ness.

Throughout this book, we will begin to see the nature of these obstacles and the process for removing them from our lives. Surprising as it may seem, people and relationships are not usually the obstacles to freedom. You really can be free without anyone changing but yourself. All of the obstacles identified in this book are things you can remove without anyone else cooperating.

Freedom is Possible

In my lifetime I have met some very free people who lived behind bars and some very bound people who lived in lavish homes. Outward circumstances have little or nothing to do with true freedom. But freedom is possible for every person. The hope of freedom really is within reach and not another frustrating myth. Freedom is achievable and not another tantalizing piece of bait to keep us running furiously on the hamster wheel of life. But we need to rightly diagnose and define our problem before we can pursue an escape route that truly provides an escape. Lasting freedom is rooted in who we are, not what we are doing. Understanding this will lead to the kind of freedom that comes from a recreated heart, not from finally discovering the right strategy.

To be free is to be able to act and react fully out of who you were designed and created to be, regardless of the circumstances of your life or the behavior of the people around you. Like the woman I mentioned earlier, so trapped in life and starved for freedom, I invite you to join me on a journey over the next several chapters, to find a way out. Decide for yourself if it is possible. Consider, perhaps, that your own fear or cynicism may be connected to some of the various traps and snares we will expose.

CHAPTER 3

WHO ARE WE?

"I can't explain myself, I'm afraid, sir," said Alice,
"because I'm not myself, you see."
— Lewis Carroll, ALICE in Wonderland

"Once upon a time, there was a woman who discovered
she had turned into the wrong person."
— Anne Tyler, Back When We Were Grown Ups

Unlike the acrobat child in the parable, nothing as dramatic as falling off a wagon and being "adopted" by strangers may have happened to us in our life. But the truth is, from birth, all of us have been raised by someone other than our real Father. The people who did raise us, attempting to pick us up along the path of life despite our own fears and insecurities, no doubt did their best to show us who we are and train us in the ways of "working the earth", but the keys to our desire and our destiny can only be given to us by our True Father.

Haven't you ever had those faint memories or yearnings, as if you had forgotten something valuable and couldn't quite remember what it was? Haven't you had to fight back the desires and urges to push beyond the limits of the life you know – to discover something outside the fields you plow every day? Or, if you have lived long enough, haven't you had to swallow hard and press down the desires you once had about life, fun and adventure, until it seemed as if you never had them in the first place?

We get in the car one more day ... we sit down at the desk or pick up the phone ... or we trudge into the conference room one more time in an endless effort to work the fields we have been trained to plow. But eventually the desire within us weakens and seems less real and less possible. We train ourselves to extinguish it before it gets us in trouble: in trouble with someone else who expects us to be who we have always been, or in trouble with our own conscience for trying things we have no business trying or being someone we have no business being.

But, what if we *are* that child of great expectations, placed here to live out something deposited within us? What if that appetite we seem to have for greatness is actually part of how we are designed? What if that dream we had when we were a kid – that someday we would become a great basketball player, doctor or musician, and that the world would be a better place because we were in it – what if that dream were rooted in a reality about us that transcended the fantasy?

> *"We often become deceived about our true identity ... it is amazing how we actually cooperate in this process of becoming someone else. Understanding why and how we cooperate will help us significantly as we define and take our first steps toward real freedom."*

At this point, many might say, "Don't get my hopes up. I finally put that to rest and have been able to move on." Maybe you silenced the voice of your dreams years ago, or maybe just recently. If so, then resurrecting those thoughts will irritate you. You might be thinking, "I don't believe in those fantasies any more" or you might say, "I finally became a realist. Why should I frustrate myself with stories that will never come true?" – as if those dreams are like Santa Claus or the Easter Bunny and it is time to put away childish things.

Our friend the acrobat gradually surrendered over the years. It didn't happen in a moment or even overnight. There were moments stacked upon more moments that contributed to the process. Step by step, he began to believe he was a farmer. It was a lifetime of quenching that fire, a lifetime of extinguishing that desire, and a lifetime of convincing himself that he should not pursue desires that he believed could not be fulfilled.

One more day ... one more row ... one more step ... you never really ask the question out loud, but it is answered a little more with each day. No, you cannot have what you desire. No, you cannot be who you think you are. Yes, you must become something else – some*one* else – or others will be disappointed or even angry with you. We may not learn to plow a field, but we do learn to focus on the earth. We learn to tend the planet and become responsible citizens, adding to the list of expectations each day: feed the cat, wash the car, make sure dinner is on the table and the bills are paid, answer emails, do your homework, and, by the way, don't let your husband down, or your parents, or your children. There is a price to be paid, so swallow hard, dream no more and take the next step.

Does all this sound familiar? Life is full of opportunities to turn our eyes away from who we are until we finally wake up one day and realize our life has become a rut. Our heart becomes buried in the process and sadly out of reach, unconsciously suppressed by our overburdened mind.

Freedom or Frustration?

To be able to act and react to life as the people we were created to be, we must realize something: when we focus on the earth during the course of living life, we often become deceived about our true identity. How does this happen? How can we become blinded to something so central as who we are? It is amazing how we actually cooperate in this process of becoming someone else. Understanding why and how we cooperate will help us significantly as we define and take our first steps toward real freedom.

When we look at our lives with honest scrutiny, what do we see? Dreams fulfilled? Deep satisfaction? Or do we see, instead, missed opportunities and unfulfilled expectations? How many times do we say, "I really wish I had ..." or "Why did I let myself ..."? The question our heart is really asking and answering every day is:

"How do I know who I was born to be
... and have I become that person?"

If all we can really do is discover a little more every day of what is true about us, then can we ever really know the answer to that question? There are so many things programming our perception of ourselves and telling us what to believe – things as broad in scope as our beliefs about the origin of the universe and the history of the world, and the pressures of the culture in which we live; or they can be more individual and specific like the influence of our own family, past events, memories, personal trauma and even celebration. Each of these carries the ability to program us. We begin our lives with the seeds of destiny in our hearts, but we don't always know when they've been uprooted by the experiences of life.

Who we are created to be (the children of promise, if you will) is directly connected to our true heritage. Just like the acrobat, our identity is determined by our DNA and our birthright, not by our circumstances. If we adopt the perspective that we begin as purely physical, biological beings – the result of a random connection of cells during sexual activity – then "randomness" is our source and "randomness" dictates our destiny. Instead, what if an all-powerful Being – One who spoke the universe into existence – is the real Source of our life, our beginning and our Father? What if He planned for you to be here on earth at this time and in this place and He deliberately engineered your existence? What if you were meant to fulfill His plan, His destiny, for your life?

Is it possible that your parents are the ones who "raised you", but not the ones who "thought you up?" They may have taught you, but what if they are not the ones who brought you into existence and put life into your body? Is it possible that your parents are not the source of your identity? The foundational truth supporting all Judeo-Christian thought is that we are the offspring of a spiritual Creator. Yes, we arrived on Earth via the interaction of other inhabitants of Earth, and our bodies were created to function and thrive in Earth's atmosphere, but our spirit is meant to thrive by connecting with a different sort of atmosphere – a different realm of experience.

Am I saying that our parents are not our parents? No, it is obvious that all of our body's cells came from the DNA provided by our parents, and our body developed in our mother's womb. But Kahlil Gibran turns our attention toward the true Source of life when he says that children come *through* you, but they do not come *from* you. The real question then is not,

"Where did my body come from?" but rather, "Where did my *life* come from?"

So What Happened?

I remember an article in the local newspaper that described children's perceptions and experiences of God. It was the opening story that grabbed my attention. A three year-old child looks into the crib of his newborn baby brother. As he watches his brother slowly awaken, his parents hear him utter the words, "As soon as you can talk, you need to tell me about God, I am starting to forget Him."

What is it about staring into the face of an infant that captivates us? For the most part, it is because they are, as yet, un-programmed. People like to use the word "innocent". I prefer "unaffected". We see in children the vague memory of what is true about us. It is a bit like the stirring in the heart of the young acrobat when he saw the poster of the acrobats on the wall. Something true about us, that we barely remember, is stirred and awakened. To know who we are is part memory and part new understanding. Like our friend the acrobat, we have deep primal memories of who we are by design. Often these memories are buried, covered or distorted by life and its experiences. Our present and future experiences give us an opportunity to "remember" what we never knew.

For years I have heard people make statements like this: "I always wanted to play guitar" or "I always wanted to be a dancer." Usually stated as a regret, I have heard people express many a life long desire that has remained unfulfilled. I am not referring to the fleeting desire to be like Michael Jordan when you see him play or the common wish to be a renowned actress after seeing the visibility and adulation she receives. I am not referring to the occasional interest we have in cool stuff. I am talking about our ongoing desires – the ones that express our untapped identity. You want to play guitar because music is in you and it needs to find expression. You want to dance because something unique about you could be expressed if you began to move the way you have seen other dancers move. Knowing who we are is part memory, that we experience as desire, and part new understanding or a new experience that instigates the desire. Pay attention to the things stirring in your heart. They may be vital clues to knowing who you are made to be.

a Search for Life

I went on a search to discover how modern medicine and science define "life". I recommend this search, since it will yield thought provoking results. Some great thinkers, as well as some "unusual" thinkers, have written volumes of material attempting to define and describe life. The fascinating thing is that most of the brilliant minds throughout history have not been able to agree upon this most basic aspect of human existence. Scientists, philosophers and physicians alike have been arguing these two questions for centuries: 1. "How do we define life?" and 2. "From where does life originate?" They use words like "growth" and "reproduction". They assign terms like "energy" or "metabolism" to label life. They struggle intellectually to describe what most people know instinctively.

What amazes me about this is that these great thinkers, while realizing that we can all recognize what is alive and what is not, feel compelled to define "aliveness". One of the clearest thinkers I found on this subject refers to the "*defining signs* of life", though he specifically avoids trying to identify what he calls "the mystical essence" which is life itself. The end result is that most scientifically minded people (including medical researchers) only ever address what I would call "symptoms" of life, and avoid any statements about what life actually *is*. So let's try to probe into this mystery, shall we?

The Breath of Life

Imagine being in an emergency room where you see a patient on a gurney. It is clear the patient is dead. All you see is a lifeless body. Whatever would make the body have alive-ness is missing. Consider all the emotions that come with moments like this: grief, a sense of loss, an aching sense of powerlessness – all of these are common reactions to the presence of death.

Into the oppressiveness of death something else begins to invade. Slowly, at first, a Wind blows into the room. This Wind seems to have substance to it. It is a little heavier than the air in the room and has a faint glow to it. Like the distortion of heated air in the summer, the solid objects on the other side of the Wind seem to bend, wavering. Now the Wind settles along the face and down the neck and sternum of the dead body. It seems to be concentrated along the center of the body, but it is hard to distinguish where the Wind blends into the rest of the air in the room.

Now you notice the Wind beginning to seep into the flesh. Like water soaking into a sponge, it soaks in and seems to ripple through the corpse. In fact, as it does, the corpse-like appearance seems to surrender to the light and weight of this Wind. Color comes into the flesh and suddenly the body takes a breath … a gasp … and then settles into a rhythmic breathing pattern. Movement begins and the face begins to have color and expression … then the eyes open. The body stands up and it becomes difficult to think of this as just a body, because it is now a person with a personality – a unique individual. As you look into his eyes and read the expression on his face, something seems familiar. Your mind struggles to identify what could be familiar about this stranger. In fact, it isn't until later that you realize why this person seemed so familiar.

Something about his expressions and the look in his eyes reminds you of the Wind itself. But how could a face look like a breeze? No wonder your mind couldn't make the connection: it's not logical! The mind is not made for this kind of knowing. As you continue to gaze, you realize another familiar aspect of this person. He has some indefinable quality you vaguely remember about yourself.

This man standing in front of you is now a "self". He also has a Source: this person's life was imparted to him by the Wind. That Source has not ceased to exist just because it has deposited life in this self. Could the man and the Source still be connected? No *visible* connection is evident, but this man seems so much like the Wind that blew into him, you feel certain some connection exists. The person has both a Source and a self. The self is self-contained. He carries it with him. He functions from it. It has a unique presentation and unique expressions. He can think, he can feel, he can analyze through his senses and he can make decisions. He is a self. He can even get up and walk out of the emergency room. He is no longer lifeless because He is connected to Life! You could almost say he has just been born, even though he did not arrive through his mother's womb.

Stay in this picture a moment longer and you may notice something else. Remember the feelings connected to seeing the dead man on the gurney? The feelings of loss, the feelings of powerlessness, now begin to fade. Not only do they fade, but in their place something else is stirring. *When death and all of its power fades, life and all of its power take over.*

As the man stands up, feelings arise within you. Instead of feeling powerless, you are infused with strength. Instead of the sadness that accompanies death, a sense of joy begins to arise. Instead of hopelessness, the expectation of something good stirs within you. Why is this? As death fades, so do the effects of death. More importantly, as life stirs, so do the effects of life.

Look around the room, and you will realize that the Wind that moved into the room has become the very atmosphere in this place. The Breath is in this man, but it is also in the air around him. Just as the oxygen we inhale fills the lungs and metabolizes all the way down to the cells, this Breath seems to continue to fill and flow through this man as he breathes in and out. Here in this atmosphere, he continues to breathe the Breath that made him alive. It is in him and around him.

"When we focus on changing behavior or reducing frustration, we often find ourselves unable to do either. However, when we learn what it means to seek first the life of God's Spirit, then everything else lines up."

His body, his mind, and his heart have not gone away or been replaced. Rather they have been filled. His mind flows with the Breath that entered him and it also stirs his emotions. The body that had been lifeless on the table is now flowing with a force which makes him alive. But not just physically alive, it also makes his thoughts and his heart alive. Where death had filled his brain and organs, they now flow with life. More than a cluster of cells, they become mind and passion as they are connected to this Breath. Where sickness had weakened and killed him, strength and health now flow.

This picture, in many ways, is what the Bible describes in its early chapters. Some-*thing* not alive becomes some-*one* alive because the very Breath of God infused life into his being. Adam was connected to God through the Breath that sustained him; yet he also had his own identity, separate from the Breath, but not wholly separate. This connection with God maintained his aliveness.

I realize this is somewhat of a mystical picture. It is, however, the very mystical aspect of this idea that science, medicine, philosophy and psychology all point toward, but hesitate to state overtly. It is hard to define, difficult to measure and certainly likely to be misunderstood. It is the spiritual core of the human race. This arena of life avoids definition and evades measure. The impact of it, however, is undeniable; for the evidence can be seen. It is similar to seeing trees move, though you cannot see the wind that moves them.

It is worth noting here that while science and medicine seem unable to define this thing called life, there is a trend in psychology toward accepting and acknowledging the impact of spiritual beliefs on the wellbeing and restoration of the human mind and emotions. It is especially recognized that in helping people overcome addictions, one of the most important factors for success is to help the addicted person tap into his or her spiritual roots. When spiritual life flows through people, it gives them power to overcome what they have not been able to overcome through their own mind, will, or emotional energy. This is because their spirit is their life-source, not their soul (the mind, will, and emotions). Only spiritual aliveness can fill the area they have been attempting to fill with their addictive behavior.

It is a significant principle that when we focus on changing behavior or reducing frustration, we often find ourselves unable to do either. However, when we learn what it means to seek first the life of God's Spirit, then everything else lines up. Karl Marx proclaimed that religion is the opiate of the masses: a drug which keeps people anesthetized, pacified and powerless. However, it is important to note that true *spiritual life* (which is something quite different from mere religion) actually has the power to help people overcome their battle with chemical and physical opiates. "Religion" (a person's own efforts to find their way to God through being "good" or following rituals) is a poor substitute for true spiritual power: the life of God breathed into a human being, bringing genuine transformation.

We might compare trying to live our lives without being connected to His Breath to a person trying to operate an unplugged pneumatic drill. Without the benefit of the air pumping through it, the drill becomes a primitive, powerless tool. It cannot fulfill the purpose for which it was designed.

Pierre Teilhard de Chardin said, "We are not human beings on a spiritual journey, rather we are spiritual beings on a human journey." Like an acrobat on a farming journey, our true nature results from our Source, not our circumstances. If freedom is rooted in our ability to become ourselves, then we must know that our essential nature is spiritual and we are designed to remain in connection to the Source of life.

The human race did not fall from a wagon, as the acrobat did, but we did fall from a connection. We fell from a connection to God, the Reality who made us who we are. It is important to realize that we had the *Breath* knocked out of us. We lost our source of feeling alive, our source of being who we really are. We disconnected from the One who is our Origin and knows every moment of our past, and the One who can also tell us what our future will be. We separated from the One whose presence enables us to see reality through a sense that transcends the five physical senses we currently employ. We fell from our connection to the spiritual realm of life. When we fell from that connection, we lost all those things. We lost our sense of aliveness, our sense of our true self, and our ability to perceive the world through spiritual senses.

The very beginning of life and the human race took place in an environment, an atmosphere, very different from the one we live in now. In the beginning, our physical senses were influenced by our spirit. But after the disconnect, the human mind resonated with the same frequency as the fallen world around it and knew death, decay and breakdown. Apart from the Breath, our physical senses are in a tug-of-war with our spirit. Until a person is re-infused with the Breath of God and spiritually reborn they cannot resonate with His higher frequency. Even after the spirit is reborn, the mind, will and emotions must be trained to co-operate with the spirit in order to bring our body, soul and spirit into agreement and alignment.

aDAMS' REALLY BAD DAY

How did our disconnection come about? We trace its origins back to the first humans to walk the earth. Here it is: "The Set Up." This wasn't just a bad day for Adam, but a bad day for the human race. Part of the answer to how we can become so confused about who we really are must bring us back to this day. The story in the Bible is not just about a man who broke a rule, it is the story of a man who broke a connection. When God told Adam about the Garden of Eden, He gave him one restriction. He said, "Do not eat from the tree of the knowledge of good and evil, because if you do, you will die." We will need to talk more about this in later chapters, but for now let's notice the protection in the warning. "If you do this you'll die – so don't do it." When God gives us a boundary, it is because He loves us and wants to keep us safe.

The confusion for so many is this: Adam and Eve both ate the forbidden fruit and then walked away from the tree. Their hearts were beating, they had brainwave activity, their cells were still reproducing – all the symptoms of life were intact. It would appear they did not die at all – that is, if you define life only by its symptoms and not its Source.

Though all their vital signs were intact, though they walked away from the tree, they had been disconnected from the Source, and they connected themselves to a different source. The significance of the Tree of the Knowledge of Good and Evil is that they ingested new input. The knowledge of good and evil became a new source of information for them, but a very inadequate source of life. *From that day forward, the way they lived was not by knowing a person, but by knowing the rules*. It was this shift that cut them off from the Source of life. The Breath no longer flowed in them. They still breathed and had a pulse, but "aliveness" was fading. When you hold your breath, you still have oxygen, but without continuing to inhale, your body begins to work on reserves until eventually they run out.

Let's return to our picture of the man in the emergency room. Along with life and death comes a whole package of experience: hope versus hopelessness, passion versus numbness, power versus powerlessness. Aliveness extends

"Our identity comes from our birthright, not from our behavior."

way beyond physiology. It extends into the mind and heart which makes us a living soul.

Freed by Definition

Let's look at our definition of freedom once again: *Freedom is when we can act and react in life as the person we are created to be*. This definition prompts the question, "So who ARE we?" Hopefully, the answer to that question has become clear: you are a spiritual being, created by God – THE Spiritual Being – the Source of all life. If He is our Source, then He is also the source of our true nature. More profound than the acrobat who inherited mere athletic skills, we were made to be receptacles and reflectors of the very nature of God Himself. What is true about Him is true about us – by design. We are created in His image. If only we could subtract the experiences of life that have programmed us, we would have a much better sense of who we were designed to be.

Perhaps you were not raised by a farmer. You may have been raised by a CEO, a preacher, an alcoholic or a model citizen. The problem with the people who have programmed your experiences is not that they are bad people. The problem is that they are *people*. What *kind* of people they were affected the experiences you had and what you came to believe about yourself and the life you live. The fact that they are human simply means it was impossible for them to give you the one thing you needed the most: to be connected to the Source of life.

In our core, our innermost essence, is where we answer the question, "Who are we?" When a disconnected man connects once again to the One who is his Source, that man's identity is established in that connection. Who we are is a direct result of what is at the exact center of our humanity. Here is an important truth to ponder:

Our identity comes from our birthright, not from our behavior.

One of the most important truths from the story of the acrobat is that sometimes what we do, how we feel, or how we think can deceive us about who we really are. How can this be? In our story, the young acrobat had experience after experience throughout his life which consistently supported The Big Lie. Having enough of these experiences made the lie feel true. His adopted mother's fears, the farmer's anger, even the geography and daily practice of life – each one bombarded him with persuasive input. Each served to frustrate the inborn desires he was designed to fulfill. The athletic aggression of the young acrobat would have served him well had he applied it to conquering gravity. Instead, this same inborn aggression was derailed and converted into destructive anger when applied in the wrong context. In the same way, we all have physical drives – such as the drive for food or sex – and these are designed to function in healthy ways. But when we try to satisfy them outside of their intended purpose, they become unhealthy, even destructive.

We, like the acrobat, are being programmed with input every day. But where is this programming stored? To say it is programmed into our mind is accurate, but not complete. It actually passes through the gateway of our mind and lodges deeper ... in our soul. The description in the Bible of God making man contains an intriguing image that can give us some clues about this "programmed self." It says that God *breathed the breath of life* into Adam's nostrils, and the man became *a living soul*. Remember the picture of the dead body in the emergency room? Something which was not alive became *someone* who was alive. In this picture you can see the difference between the "Breath" which made the man alive and the "soul" which became the man's vehicle to transport the Breath he had received. The spirit God breathed into him gave him life, and his life was connected to, but separate from, his Source – God.

What had been a brain was now a mind. More than a physical structure, he became a receiver, a processor, an integrator. What had been a four-chambered organ became a heart. Besides a pulse, he had passion. He wasn't just "not dead", Adam was full of aliveness. His mind and heart took in the world around him. It sorted through the input and organized what he saw. His mind and heart fueled his desires, creating urges within him. He saw things and desired them. His mind and heart suggested to him what he ought to choose, and when he did, his mind, his heart and his will interacted with the world around him. This was his soul, but not his Source.

The Breath in him and around him was his Source, his origin. It was this programmable container – his mind, his heart and his will – that made him separate and uniquely himself – separate from the Breath, but made alive by it. At this point, if we are forced to answer the question, "Who is Adam?" we must say that *who he is* comes directly from his Source. He is God's offspring. Adam is not God, but made in His image. At the *core* – the center of his being – that is who he is. But if you had the ability to ask Adam, he might answer differently. His experience of himself comes from his mind and heart. If he stubs his toe, has a muscle spasm, or just a bad day, he might waver in his answer about who he is. If he had a *really* bad day, imagine what that might do.

When Adam and Eve walked away from the tree, their choice set into motion a cycle of dying. They could have no idea in that moment, or even in the years to come, the full implications of what had just happened. They could not know what it meant for their own future, nor the unfolding future of the race which was birthed through them. Their fall had two significant and world altering effects. Both effects were devastating and both were outside their own ability to overcome. It is these two things we must learn on our journey to freedom, and it is these two things which Jesus came to overcome.

Chapter 4

What Happened? a Different Source

"Maybe we've been livin' with our eyes half open,
maybe we're bent and broken ... broken."
— Switchfoot, *Meant to Live*

"But I want it now, Daddy!"
— Veruka Salt, *Charlie and the Chocolate Factory*

LYING on the side of the road, the infant acrobat could have

no idea of the full implications of his fall. He knew, instinctively, that something terribly scary had just happened to him. What he could not know was that the whole course of his life had just changed. He had no way to know, because he had just been separated from the ones who had been the source of his knowledge up until that moment. Nor did his new "parents" know the story they had just entered. The only ones who knew were now cut off from access to their son and he was cut off from them. He had fallen from a wagon, but he had also fallen from a vital connection. Each moment that he lay there, powerless to help himself, his parents were swiftly passing into the distance, along with his intended way of life. Simultaneously, a very different way of life was approaching on the path, represented by the two strangers who would scoop him up and deliver him to their home on the farm.

TWO PROBLEMS—ONE BIG MESS

To really return to the life we are created for, we must understand what happened to it. The acrobat story gives us part of the picture, but we must complete the map so we can find our way back. As we said at the end of

Chapter Three, two things happened when Adam and Eve ate the forbidden fruit; one event with two significant impacts. When Adam walked away from the tree, he had no way of knowing everything he had just set in motion for himself and the whole human race. He just knew something scary had happened and, just like the baby acrobat, two things resulted.

First, he was disconnected from his Source, the One who made him who he was. But in Adam's case, he wasn't just cut off from his Father, he was separated from the Source of life. The second equally damaging effect was that he connected to a different, completely ineffective, source. The acrobat connected to a farmer and his wife, but Adam and Eve (and the whole human race after them) connected to something far worse. They didn't connect to another person, they connected to themselves. By looking to a source of knowledge other than God, Adam tried to become his own source. He chose the path of self-reliance, setting a course of failure for the whole human race. Taking the Knowledge of Good and Evil into his own hands (literally!) meant that it was up to Adam to figure out what was wrong and up to him to make it right.

The problem wasn't just that Adam was inadequate (though that was true); the problem was that Adam was … well … himself. Connecting to yourself as a source is like trying to reach under your own feet and pick yourself up off the ground. Without any leverage from an external source, you will fail.

I play the guitar and when I was a teenager I got my first amplifier. I noticed that there was an extra outlet on the back of the amplifier, so I thought, "Cool! I'll just plug my guitar into the amplifier and then plug the amplifier into itself (via the extra outlet) and then I can take it anywhere." It took me just a minute to realize the obvious: the amplifier couldn't power itself because it needed an external power source. If only Adam had the benefit of that electronic illustration, who knows, things might have been different? Maybe not.

Here is another illustration. If your car's gas tank is halfway full, you cannot fill the tank by siphoning gas from the same tank. In the same way, Adam could not fill his tank with the contents of his own tank. But the consequences went further than just feeling "empty". Adam's whole *way* of life changed: his way of feeling alive, his way of understanding, his way of taking in and knowing truth, his way of relating to others and even his way of relating to himself. What happened would be the equivalent of disconnecting a computer from a power cable and connecting it to only a data cable. Data alone cannot sustain power, but if data is all that is available, you will try to draw power from it.

Understanding what changed, beginning with Adam and Eve, is very important when trying to understand how to change it back. Unfortunately, part of what changed was man's *way* of learning the very things we are talking about. It is difficult to find your glasses when you don't have your glasses. In the same way, our need to see accurately is muddied by the very problem we desire to solve. One of the reasons we end up in bondage to our bad definitions of freedom is because of the self-reliance we inherited from Adam and Eve when they disconnected from God. Before going further, let me re-state the two problems:

Our condition as a result of the fall

1) People are born into this world disconnected from the Source of true life.

2) Man has connected to himself as his own source.

These two problems are connected and actually feed each other. Each makes the other a little more complicated. In fact, these two problems, unresolved, might even keep you from getting free as you read this chapter.

Like the driver I described who was trying to change lanes, the problem can be amplified by the attempted solution. These two effects of the fall create the frustrating cycle inherent in the human race. The knowledge of good and evil leaves incomplete people in charge of their own solutions. We think we see what's wrong and we think we see what would fix it. We think we know because we've connected to the knowledge of good and evil as our new source. However, if our definitions are inaccurate, then we are already stuck.

Disconnected

Turn off the phone. Leave the television silent. Don't play your iPod. Stay away from the internet. Just sit still … for a few minutes. Do you feel anxiety start to rise? Are you uncomfortable even reading about five minutes of unplugged life? What is that feeling? – that sense of nagging discomfort when we begin to remove our distractions? What is that anxiety when we begin to lay down any or all of the opiates of the masses that we have developed? Try it for a few minutes. Put the book down and see how long you can keep still ... no music ... no stimulus.

People tell me they feel guilty when they do nothing. People tell me they just don't like to be alone with themselves. This is universal. In the silence, in the stillness, awareness begins. And awareness is uncomfortable, some would even say painful or frightening. This is the universal awareness that we are *disconnected*. It feels stark. It feels lonely. Throw a few more adjectives at it. Bottom line: it feels empty. That's how disconnection feels. When that which gave us life is cut off – and all the experiences associated with aliveness – here come the experiences associated with death. Given enough time, heaviness, powerlessness, sadness and guilt will show up. It's no wonder that most people don't want to slow down! It's not surprising they don't want to turn off their gadgets. They might become more aware of their emptiness.

"The problem was shame – the dawning awareness that, 'Something is wrong with me.'"

Let me give you another name for this universal disconnection: sin. When Adam and Eve walked away from the tree, they weren't just guilty and being punished, they were disconnected. I am not saying that all the feelings I just mentioned are sinful, I am saying that an accurate and more helpful understanding of sin points us to the emptiness of the human heart, not just a list of bad behaviors. In Spanish, the word "*sin*" literally means *without*. We are without connection to our source. This is problem number one.

Clearly, Adam and Eve disobeyed, but their disobedience has not been our problem. Instead, the problem is the condition that we all inherited from them: sin, emptiness and all the feelings and behaviors that arise out of emptiness. It feels horrible to be empty. This leads us to problem number two.

KNOWLEDGE OF GOOD AND EVIL

If I have become my own source, I am immediately aware of how empty I have become. This knowledge feels stark and miserable and I want it to go away. I look for relief, but discover that since I am my own source, I must now come up with my own solution. I must invent my own version of good to overcome this miserable feeling of emptiness. It is now up to me to fix me.

The first deceptive "fix" seems easy, yet it leads me down a self-destructive path. It plays out like this: I don't like the way I feel and I don't like the growing awareness that something is wrong with me, so I try to convince myself that the problem is not me but rather something else … someone else … *anything* besides me. Now at least I feel a little bit better – a quick fix, for now. This sets up a very dangerous trap. This person can get no help for the real problem until he defines the problem accurately – until he is willing to look at the very thing from which he has turned. These "quick fixers" must eventually acknowledge that something is wrong with *them*. And all of their instincts tell them not to do this. Nobody wants to acknowledge something is wrong with them. The human being is the only creature that can lie to itself and believe its own lie. This mental contortion is a direct result of the universal problems we have just described. The feeling of disconnectedness is so strong and painful, we will do anything to make it go away, even blame the people we love most in order to ease our pain.

We observe this destructive response in the account of Adam and Eve. We read that they knew they were naked and they were ashamed. The problem wasn't nakedness, they were naked before. The problem was shame – the dawning awareness that, "Something is wrong with me." The very next step? They exercised their limited knowledge of good and thought they ought to hide. So they hid. Then they began to cover themselves with leaves. Hiding, hiding, hiding. It is our instinctive response to the awareness of just how empty we are. This is the beginning of our ability to lie to ourselves and believe it. This is not just a mental exercise, it is instinct.

When the body undergoes a major trauma, such as an injury or some horrifying circumstance, an amazing thing happens. The nervous system sets up an elaborate reaction to protect the mind and body from the full effect of the trauma: shock. Shock is an involuntary protective response. It prevents the person from being overwhelmed by the full impact of the trauma. The nervous system shuts down so that the pain is numbed and the mind goes into filter mode to keep out overwhelming information.

When our perceptions feed us too much painful input, then our perceptual mechanisms immediately start to minimize, or even exclude, the overwhelming input. If we are not careful, we could be affected by this very phenomenon even as we are trying to make the point about our disconnectedness. We may tune out this very discussion because we do not want to hear. Some traumatic or painful aspects of this discussion may shut down our system.

"If our core problem is that we are disconnected from our Source, then how can we clean ourselves up?"

The first part of the story of Adam and Eve is the story of how a non-living thing became a living person. But this part of the story is about a traumatic event. Something happened to the two of them that was devastating to them and it continues to be devastating to us. Because it is devastating, our mind can quickly shut down and begin to minimize input.

STUCK IN THE CYCLE

Here is the cycle: something is wrong with us. It feels unsettling, at best, and overwhelming at its worst. Our system goes to work to relieve this overwhelming sensation and hides from us the truth of what is wrong. In our deceived state, we set about fixing everything, and everyone, except the thing that most needs to be fixed: ourselves. As we set about trying to fix things we can actually do more damage by multiplying the negative effect and increasing the potential for pain. The condition worsens, the defenses strengthen, the lie grows stronger and the emptiness grows deeper.

This is a little bit like the person who doesn't want to go to the doctor for fear of what they may find out. The fear keeps them from having an accurate picture and if the condition they are avoiding worsens, they are avoiding the very help they need while their condition deteriorates. The more they fear the doctor, the worse things get ... and the cycle goes on. *a watered down version of whose*

The truth is we are in bondage to being ~~ourselves. We are stuck being us.~~ We *were* cannot lift our own body off the ground. We cannot fill our own emptiness. *meant* And built into this emptiness is a "way of knowing" that makes it very unlikely *to be* we will even see our problem, much less agree that the problem exists.

WHAT ABOUT THE BAD STUFF?

By now you might be asking yourself: "If sin is the emptiness of the human heart, then what about smoking and drinking and having illicit sex? I thought sin was the stuff we need to clean up in our lives so we can please God." But if our core problem is that we are disconnected from our Source, then how can we clean ourselves up? It would be like expecting a self-cleaning oven to clean itself without being plugged into the electrical power.

I can hear you asking: "What about the bad stuff, though? What about what I thought sin was? You know, the smoking, drinking and chewing thing. Are you trying to say that those things aren't sin?" Those things may be the outward manifestation of sin, because [sin is a condition before it becomes ✳ a behavior.] The things that people do that we think of as sinful are a result of emptiness. No one likes to feel empty. In fact, most people ache to feel alive. This is why the young acrobat in our story needed some way to express what was in him, even though he still didn't know who he really was. He found himself exploding with anger, but the anger was not the main problem, it was the result of a deeper problem.

Behaviors that we have thought of as sinful, though they are problematic, are not the problem. They are the result of the problem. When people feel empty or dead inside, they will naturally try to find ways to feel alive and fulfilled. So what does it take to *feel* alive when life isn't in you? Well, it depends on who raised you – a farmer? ... an alcoholic? ... or a workaholic?

The things that people turn to in order to feel alive are as varied as their life circumstances. Our history and experience come together to convince us where we will find life. One family believes wealth will bring them life, another believes it will come from power and influence.

Some people turn to drugs or alcohol to numb the feeling of deadness inside and to try to find a moment or two of aliveness. Some people turn to sex or other risky behaviors. Some believe their job will make them feel fulfilled. People become convinced that all these things can give them life. Still others will turn to religion, the priesthood, service, or any number of good things. The people Jesus corrected the most were those who were trying to fill their emptiness with religious performance. Are these things sin? No, remember, sin is not a set of behaviors, it is the condition of being separated from God. Anything we turn to in order to fill the absence of God from our heart is simply a symptom of sin. Some of these things look really good, others look really bad.

One of the stumbling blocks that can prevent us from connecting to our Creator sounds like this: "What I have done is not as bad as Hitler ..." or "I haven't really done anything that bad ..." I can think of a lot of religious answers that follow that type of reasoning, but here is the bottom line: don't ask how what you have done compares to the lives of others. Ask this instead: "Am I alive? Am I connected to the One who is the living stream of Breath that makes aliveness happen?"

The problem with the human race is not simply a matter of bad behavior. The problem with the human race is emptiness. We are empty of the thing that makes us most who we are and makes us feel fully alive. We are empty and it drives us all towards something, anything that might soothe the uncomfortable awareness that something is not right. We were born by and from the breath of God. We remained connected to the breath of God for a short time, then we fell ... off the wagon, out of the garden, we fell. We unplugged. Has it resulted in bad behavior? Absolutely. It has also resulted in a lot of good behavior that is motivated and driven by emptiness.

If Jesus came to earth and just told us to behave better, a lot of us would try. Some might do better than others. Some might even do pretty well, much of the time. But eventually, the futility of trying to "straighten up and fly right" would win out. How do you try to fill your own empty heart? What could you possibly fill it with that wasn't already yours? Remember, the problem is that what you presently have is empty. Fill up with that and empty plus empty still equals empty. If you are driving down the road and the gas in your tank is nearly gone, you do not stop alongside another driver whose tank is also empty. You certainly do not pull over and tap into your own gas-less tank in order to fill up. Nor do you try to improve your driving skills to replenish the tank. We would all recognize the foolishness of those options. Great driving will not fill your tank and bad driving will not make it emptier. The solution to an empty gas tank is to stop at a gas station that has a supply of something that you do not. You then hook up to that supply and transfer to your car what it has been missing. Problem solved – you are no longer empty.

Good analogy

"... something whispers to you that you were made for more than you have known."

The solution for the human race is similar. How do you free yourself from who you are? You must go somewhere where you can connect to someone "not-you" – a "not you" who has something that can fill you. Not just empty calories, but something to fill you up with aliveness. What we get from God is a re-connect to the Source of aliveness.

YOUR ACROBAT MOMENT

You may have had your "acrobat moment" years ago, or it might be happening as you read this book. You begin to realize your parents may not be your parents. Sure, they raised you, but you have always known that something else was burning in your heart. Maybe you haven't known it logically, but this isn't the sort of thing that the mind is made for knowing. Something in your heart, in your awareness, something that surfaces on some days and other days remains hidden … something whispers to you that you were made for more than you have known. This whispered conversation captures your heart with more than just information. Instead, it confirms a growing awareness: you have another dad – not the one who raised you, but the One who gave you life – and He is offering you life again. His offer is not made in a demanding way, nor does He condemn you in anger. He has missed you and He wants you to consider joining the family.

It is a choice between two worlds: what you have always known on your left and this stranger who tells you He is your father on the right. Logic doesn't help here. The things stirring in your soul are both familiar and foreign. Familiar in a deeply primal sense, but foreign in that you cannot know anything about this new family. All you know is that you are faced with not just *a* choice, but *the* choice – the one you've been waiting for. All of your life you have been in bondage to *you* and you didn't even know it up until this moment. This is the one choice that offers a way out, or is it a way in? He is offering a way back into the family, a way back into the atmosphere filled with life and designed to fill you. He offers you a life that is re-connected to the beautiful, life-giving connection Adam lost – and He is offering it for free.

Forgiveness

How could God offer it for free? Isn't there a cost involved? Isn't there a price to be paid for sin? That's what you've heard and that is correct. But you have also heard that sin is sex, drugs and rock and roll, or whatever list of behaviors you were given. So in our mind, the price is like bail money. Jesus paid the legal equivalent of my offense to get me out of jail. He paid my way out, so I must now live my life to pay Him back, right? Well, here is the beauty of forgiveness. We have spent the last several pages stating that sin is my condition, my nature, not just my behavior. Yes, that condition resulted in behavior, but most people reading this have not done enough bad stuff to merit the death sentence. I'd like you to understand, once and for all, what you can really be forgiven of.

I have said repeatedly that because of our lost connection life was no longer in us. So what was in us? Death! Death has been in us. This is why our quest to feel alive is so intense. No one wants to feel dead. It is this death in me that makes it so uncomfortable, even painful, for me to be alone with *me*. Jesus died to exchange the life in Him for the death in me. *He died to forgive me for who I am, not just what I've done.*

Here is what this means: He sets me free from *who I have become* and not just the habits of my past. In forgiving me for who I have become, Jesus opens the door to make a connection again to the Source of life. I can be born again! But this second time I am born from the breath of my Father and not just the womb of my mother. I am reconnected. It is important that we know we are not just invited back into the family – we are reconnected to our Source! We are made spiritual men and women again.

When you open up and receive this for the first time then your feet have finally hit the path. Every other attempt at freedom has been waiting for this first step. Your definitions will begin to come into focus and you will see, perhaps for the first time, why your other attempts have not worked. Your drive to be free has brought you to this. Finally free from yourself, you'll look up and begin to realize things can never be the same. Your eyes begin to focus and you see, though blurry at first, that everything around you has changed.

CHAPTER 5

THE NATURE OF THE WAR

"Buckle your seatbelt, Dorothy, 'cause Kansas is going bye-bye."

"Why, oh why, didn't I take the blue pill?"
— Cypher, *The Matrix*

Suppose for a minute that all that I've said so far

makes sense to you and you made a decision. You decided, like the acrobat, to reconnect to your true source. Though it seemed strange and foreign to you at first, deep inside you sense your true self reawakening. From this moment on things have changed. Oh yes, they have changed! Like our friend the acrobat, you don't realize at this point just how much. For him, everything changed at once, but he could only learn one thing at a time. You have made a choice that affects much more than you can imagine. You might think you just became a church-goer. Some would say you "got religion". You may have watched others go through this change. Now, because it is your own experience, you realize that you have taken a first step into freedom. When you take this step two very important things happened to you that you must become aware of right away:

1. **You have just changed your citizenship.** The Bible makes it clear that you were translated from one kingdom into another (Colossians 1:13). When you were "translated" you were moved into, and made compatible with, a kingdom unlike anything you've known before. You just became a citizen of a spiritual realm.

2. You have stepped into a war zone. As a citizen of this new kingdom, you should know that the enemy of freedom just took notice of you.

I must state directly at this time that freedom for the human race is viciously opposed. I don't just mean that it is difficult, though it is. Nor do I just mean that serious obstacles arise along the way, although they do. I mean that there is an enemy who has declared an all-out war against your freedom. Sound a little extreme? Then just see what happens when you set your mind to really pursue freedom. Don't be afraid. I know that sounds extreme, well, it is pretty extreme, but it's going to be all right. The good news is that, even though you stepped into a war zone, you stepped in on the winning side. The sooner you learn your way around and learn about the war, the sooner you can enjoy winning.

This war against your freedom has been going on for years before you even knew about it. It started before you were born. It was raging around you all the time, you just couldn't see it. No wonder change was so hard and freedom was so evasive! Now that you are aware of the war, you stand a much better chance of engaging effectively. You should know that this war you have joined is fought on two fronts simultaneously. The primary front is fought inside you: it is the battle to become yourself. Win here, and you will always win on the other front: the battle to return to the purpose God originally designed for your life. That battle rages all around you. When you become who you were created to be, you will discover how to flow in your purpose as God's representative here on earth, and you will learn how to exercise the dominion He gave you over the enemy of freedom. If you lose the battle on the inside of you, you will always struggle to win the one on the outside.

Here is a paradox: as you are winning the battle on the inside, sometimes it might appear that you are losing the one on the outside. When things outwardly are contrary to your desires or preferences, yet you maintain peace on the inward front, then you have gained ground. The enemy of your freedom will constantly try to provoke you to surrender some territory in the battle. Jesus said that when someone strikes your face and you turn the other cheek, then that is evidence that you are a child of God – because He is kind and merciful, even to those who don't deserve it! You are a citizen of His kingdom. He wasn't recommending that you become a passive punching bag, but He knows that when someone else's behavior pushes you to react, you have given them control over your emotions and that is a disempowered position. King Solomon wrote: "He that is slow to anger is better than the mighty; and he that rules his spirit than he that takes a city." When you can take dominion over your own emotions, you become mighty in battle. The inward battle and the outward battle are related to one another, and both are connected to your freedom. Here's some good news: just by entering into the war on purpose, you are already freer than you were before you engaged.

THE BIG LIE

She was angry, probably the angriest person I have ever met. Don't take that the wrong way, because she had every reason to be angry. I think you would have been too, if you had lived her life. Imagine everything that could go wrong in a little girl's life and hers was worse. The men in her family, her father included, had all treated her in ways that no man should treat anyone. Her mother, aware of the abuse, turned a blind eye to her daughter's plight. She allowed her own fear to trump any motherly, protective instinct she might have had. The little girl was all alone in the hands of fearful, sick humans. You would have become angry too.

Finally, in her mid-thirties, she found her way into my counseling office. I was a beginner and (though I would never have told her this) I was a bit intimidated. Her anger was palpable and ever-present. It filled every room she entered. She had multiple compulsive behaviors and she carried herself like a line-backer ready to attack at the first sign of danger. To her, danger was when anybody tried to get close. She carried none of the trappings of femininity. She wore no make up, just a scowl. She let her hair hang un-tended and un-styled. The way she dressed was also quite plain, often wearing only jeans and a nondescript T-shirt. Her countenance and her posturing attempted to hide the fact that she was, indeed, a woman.

Her anger and fear were contagious. In fact, she had caught it from her own family. In the course of acting and reacting toward others in her life, she made many other people angry as well. Her quick temper hurt and confused others as she lashed out at those whose greatest offense was trying to befriend her. She could chase away people whose only intent was to show her kindness. Moreover, she could elicit negative reactions from some very positive people.

In our early days together we worked on anger and addictive behaviors. We worked on the roots of anger as well as on understanding and managing the cycles of her anger. I did everything I knew (and learned a lot in the process), to try to help tame the monster inside her. We had lots of opportunities to see her anger play itself out in her life and often in the room between us. Bit by bit, it subsided. Her compulsive behaviors began to loosen their grip. One day I decided to draw attention to "The Big Lie" – the one that had gained control and was squeezing the life out of her.

I looked her square in the eyes and I said, "You know, God made you a woman."

Her look began to change. I'd seen it before – the flush in her cheeks, the tightness in her jaw – her anger was stirring. "Don't you *ever* say that to me!" she said through gritted teeth.

I probably should have backed away, but I didn't. I began again. "I know you don't like to hear it, but God made you a woman," I countered.

Now the lid was off. Her face was a deep red and her jaw clenched tightly as she uttered these words: "Women are weak," she growled, "and women are victims, and I will *not be one.*"

Now The Big Lie was out because she spoke it. It came out with the force of years of experience that made it all seem so true. It came out with the associated pain and fear that had planted the lie deep in the recesses of her heart. It came out and hung in the air, for both of us to examine. There it was. She thought it was the ultimate truth, but I knew it was a lie – not the pain or fear, those were real. It was the meaning she had attached to her experience that became The Big Lie for her. Her painful experiences had become attached to her female-ness and so she was determined to throw them both out with the proverbial bathwater. She *could not* live with the pain of her victimization so she *would not* live with her womanhood. In her mind and heart, the two were one.

I began to dig a hole under The Big Lie. I hoped the whole thing would collapse one day. I told her again that she was a woman. Her biology was undeniable. I also told her she was victimized, not because she was a woman, but because her family was sick and they were wounded themselves. I reminded her that she knew some women who were both feminine and strong. I pointed out the protections she now had as a grown up: that she was stronger and lived thousands of miles from her family. It was now safe to be herself.

"The kind of truth that makes people free is when our minds and our hearts begin to agree with God and we begin to see things the way He does. It re-makes us. It transforms us."

For weeks this went on. I offered a steady presentation of contradictory evidence, submitted for her consideration. I had begun to wonder if we were getting anywhere when my phone rang one day and she was on the other end, calling from work. She began to relay to me a story I will never forget.

She was sitting at her desk, minding her own business, when she had some strange sensations begin in her body. "So I got up," she said, "and went to the ladies' room. When I got there I discovered my period had started."

"Hmmm," I said, in my best professional counselor's voice. Wondering why she had called me with this news, I went on, "So you are calling me because …" I waited. Surely, at this stage in her life, she didn't need me to tell her how to handle her menstrual cycle.

She stated what I had yet to comprehend: "I'm calling you because I have never had a period before."

Remember, this was a woman in her mid-thirties. The Big Lie had not just affected her emotions and her habits, it had affected her organs and her chemistry – her body had refused to be a woman too! Yet, as her heart began to agree with God's original design, her body followed suit. This illustrates the truth God states in Proverbs 23:7: "As a man thinks in his heart, so is he." – *she*, in this case.

In the days that followed, I kept hearing in my mind the words of Jesus:

"You can know the truth, and the truth will make you free." The kind of truth that makes people free is not simply the correct alignment of orthodox doctrine. It is not a mental agreement with accurate theology. The kind of truth that makes people free is when our minds *and our hearts* begin to agree with God and we begin to see things the way He does. It re-makes us. It transforms us.

The war against freedom is a war against what we see, what we believe to be ultimate truth, and a war against our *way* of seeing and our *way* of knowing. It takes place within us and it takes place around us. As long as this woman believed The Big Lie, she treated people around her in accordance with The Big Lie. As she did, she wounded or angered others, fueling whatever version of The Big Lie they believed. As we come to know the truth – what God sees and *how He sees it* – we begin to treat others in accordance with the truth. As we do, they too can come to know the Truth and the truth can make them free.

THE BATTLEGROUND

The war fought to win America's independence from the British was very different from the war waged against the Taliban following September 11, 2001. Comparing the two wars, the terrain was different, the nature of the enemy was different, and the degree of public support was different. Therefore, each war required a unique battle strategy. A wise warrior knows the nature of his enemy, the terrain the battles will be fought on, and the strategies that most fit his analysis of these factors. The war for our personal freedom is a specific kind of war with a specific terrain. Our enemy knows our strengths and has targeted our weaknesses, and he has developed his strategies accordingly.

Below is a map of the territory where this battle plays out. We must see the relationship between the inward war and the outward war. They are two sides of one coin and must be fought simultaneously because each affects the other. Take a moment to consider and understand the map below, because we'll be referring to it often.

Action → Experience

Our actions often create or lead to our experience. Much of what we experience in life is directly related to our own actions. Though not always, many of our consistent experiences are connected to choices we make, or behaviors we regularly participate in. What leads to our actions?

Choice → Action → Experience

For every action we commit, we make a choice. At times, we choose deliberately and consciously; other times, almost instantaneously and with little or no conscious thought. In either case, choice plays some role in our actions. So where do our choices come from?

Desire → Choice → Action → Experience

Our choices are directly connected to our desires. We can respond out of an immediate desire or an ongoing desire. I desire cake, I eat. Indirectly, I desire comfort and cake might provide this, so I eat. Because I desire comfort, I make a choice based on this desire. We cannot act contrary to our desires for extended periods of time. Sometimes our desires are hierarchical e.g. I desire health *and* I desire cake. Ultimately, the one I desire most will win out. Desire always eventually leads to choices. Where do our desires come from?

Perception → Desire → Choice → Action → Experience

It is crucial to recognize the role of perception in this roadmap. Because I desire comfort, I am drawn toward that which I *perceive* will provide comfort. When I don't feel like a man, my desires turn toward that which I *perceive* will make me experience masculinity. The power of our desires can be harnessed by the shifting of our perceptions. Every good advertising campaign is based on this principle. My perception is designed to link my true self to my desires. When my perceptions are off, the whole roadmap can work against me, instead of for me. When I perceive accurately who I am, my desires express my true identity.

Identity → Perception → Desire → Choice → Action → Experience

Our perception or beliefs have the power to separate our experience from our true identity. An acrobat can think and feel like a farmer; a man can have thoughts and feelings that are completely unlike his true identity. The fruit of all this then leads to our impact on others and on our valued relationships.

Identity → Perception → Desire → Choice → Action → Experience → Impact

This progression can become circular when our experience and impact support and strengthen our perceptions.

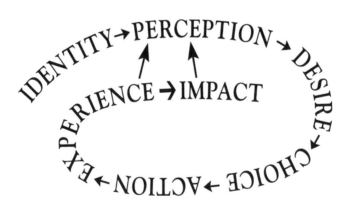

For example, when a gambler wins an immediate payoff, the experience will increase the perception that he can win. As a result, his desire to gamble grows, causing him to make more choices which perpetuate that behavior and the cycle continues. On the positive side, if a person who fears downhill skiing does it anyway and has a great experience, then that experience increases the perception that the outcome is not as bad as she feared, so future choices will be based on this new perception. This is how patterns of thought and behavior become dominant.

Let's take the woman whose story was told earlier in this chapter. Here is where the progression took her:

Perception: Femininity is dangerous.
Desire: I do not want to be hurt.
Choice(s): I will protect myself.
Action(s): Drugs and alcohol, anger and violence
Experience: I am not hurt in the same way again, but people are afraid of me (which hurts).
Impact: I then hurt others, harming my interpersonal relationships.
Perception: I am dangerous.

And the cycle goes around again.

This is the map of the territory where the battles are fought. If my perceptions can be influenced, then the whole chain is affected. This can work *for me* or *against me*. The more I perceive the truth, the more my choices lead me to experience freedom. The more I am deceived, the more I am led into bondage.

Referring to the diagram let me point out one trap before we address how the war takes place. Often when we try to pursue freedom in our lives, we pursue it at the level of choice or action. When we do this, we significantly underestimate or even ignore the power of perception and desire. When we try to change our actions and choices without changing our perception, we set up a war within us that we are unlikely to win.

"Having accurate definitions and knowing the truth are foundational for freedom. If I were going to try to ruin your life, I would wage a war against how you perceive and define reality."

Desires are hierarchical. This simply means that some desires will either trump, or be trumped, by other desires. I desire to be healthy. I desire ice cream with hot fudge. One of these will win. I desire to pass my class, but I also desire to run around with my friends the night before the big test. One of these will win and the winner will always be based on perceptions. Perception has influencing power. Perception is the driving force in the whole progression of the map.

Every good advertising executive knows this, whether this language is used or not. Advertisements, as well as other media messages, are designed specifically to impact the consumer's perceptions, moving them in the direction of desire. If those two things are moved, then the whole flow of the map follows. As a result, we decide to violate our budget and purchase a new gadget.

Perception is an unbelievably powerful force which can drive our progression toward or away from freedom. What perception? Well, the perception of reality in general, but especially the perception of yourself and of God. If you perceive yourself to be a failure, what are the odds you will make choices and actions that bring success? If you perceive yourself to be a farmer, how likely are you to be a successful acrobat? In the same way, if you perceive God to be harsh and angry, the odds are that you will make life choices and react in situations according to your picture of God. If you perceive God to be distant and uninvolved, your choices and actions will reflect this as well. Because perception is the driver, having accurate definitions and knowing the truth are foundational for freedom. If I were going to try to ruin your life, I would wage a war against how you perceive and define reality.

THE WAR AGAINST DEFINITIONS

Yad Vashem, the Holocaust museum in Jerusalem, traces the pathway of an unfolding period in world history that resulted in the tragic mass murder of millions of Jews. People who should have known better participated in the brutal and horrifying treatment of Jewish people that changed the face of a continent.

In Yad Vashem, the tour itself illustrates how a culture followed an ever descending pathway toward accepting that which is unacceptable. It began with a war, waged in print, against definitions. Newspaper articles with a prejudicial slant and political cartoons, depicting Jews as dangerous or despicable, were all part of an all-out campaign that began to change public opinion toward the Jewish people. Ultimately, the campaign defined Jews as a threat to society and less than human. Once this new definition was established, it was frighteningly easy to move public opinion in Europe toward cooperation, and then down the road to the Holocaust.

Today we call it propaganda: the onslaught of published material and other mass communication that shapes public opinion, promoting specific agendas or outcomes. The Nazis began their war against the Jewish people by using the weapon of propaganda to spread false information and form inaccurate perceptions in the minds of the general public. It was not just a war against information, it was a war against truth. It was a war against a *way* of knowing.

Today we fight a similar war. People who should know better participate in the war. An intentional and vicious war rages against both our understanding and our *way* of understanding the truth, in order to keep men and women enslaved. Men who are called spiritual leaders molest and rape their parishioners, tainting our image of spiritual leaders as well as our trust in them. Politicians pursue personal gain and private agendas with little or no regard for how it affects the people they serve or how it undermines the very government designed to protect the people.

The propaganda against our definitions has been slick, creating counterfeit definitions that trap us. Our whole culture is involved in the propaganda war. At this point in our history, we have arrived at culturally accepted definitions which lead us into worldviews that keep us marching steadily into our own bondage. Things that were once absolutely off limits on television are commonplace today. Things once considered private, like sexual issues, are now public spectacle. The moral boundaries of our culture have been redefined.

Even worse, many of these definitions and worldview issues make us averse to the things we need most in order to be free. Like a patient who fears needles but desperately needs an injection, we may be resisting, even opposing, the very thing that can help us the most. Imagine that you are in great pain and you go see a doctor to get some relief. Anxious for help, you are dismayed when the doctor refuses to tell you the diagnosis. "It would be judgmental for me to say what is wrong with you," he says. Then he asks you the strangest question. "What kind of medicine would you prefer?" Your symptoms and your intense discomfort tell you that something is definitely wrong, but you realize that you don't know enough to self-diagnose, let alone prescribe your own medicine! You reply, "Well, Doc, first tell me what's wrong with me." He appears uncomfortable, squirms a bit, and says, "I didn't say anything was wrong with you, did I? I would really hate for you to feel judged by me." Now you are really annoyed. "Look, I feel terrible! Just tell me what kind of medicine I need to take." "Well," he stutters, "not everyone likes every kind of medicine, so what kind of medicine do you prefer?"

You can see how ridiculous this approach would be. But in a similar way, the condition of our spirit and soul requires an accurate diagnosis and a compassionate, specific treatment that will cure the problem. When our soul is in pain, we need someone to love us enough to tell us the truth so that we can be restored to health to enjoy what Jesus called "abundant life".

However, these days it is no longer acceptable to point out and label destructive behavior. It is considered intolerant to do so. We have been passive in the subtle war of propaganda waged against those things that we most need. We face an ongoing onslaught of information vying for a place in our minds. Some of it is accurate, but much of it is inaccurate or even deceptive. Some things we see with clarity, some are less obvious.

Communication: The Programming of Our Minds

Communication. We take it for granted because we are immersed in it every day. Like oxygen, we are surrounded by it and infused with it. It seems like such a simple thing, both because of its familiarity and the assumption most of us have that we are pretty good at it. But let me say as someone who has done countless hours of marriage counseling, we are not very good at it.

The great enemy of communication is assumption in all its forms and practices. We assume we understand and we also assume we have been understood. We assume everyone is like us or we assume no one else is like us. One of the greatest obstacles is when we assume that we have the complete picture or context in regard to what we are communicating. Like the common saying of our day, "We don't know what we don't know."

Therefore, we assume we know everything we need to know and proceed. Tucked within this assumption is one of the most distorting obstacles: different contexts call for different *ways of knowing*. Don't miss this. If you miss this concept, then you might miss the other ideas in this book completely. This is the concept that often keeps husbands and wives from coming into unity. I'll say it again. We have different *ways* of knowing.

This idea is one of the most important concepts you will read in these pages. Don't go too quickly here. Take time to let this truth settle in. This idea – that we have differing *ways* of knowing – is the lens through which you will have the capacity to see many other ideas. It is the prism through which light enters and then is separated into distinct colors.

Ways of Knowing

Since this is so important, let me state it directly: we as people have a variety of *ways* of knowing things. If we do not recognize these ways or channels of knowing, then we may miss some of the most important "knowings" in our life.

A friend of mine was faced with the all important decision of choosing his life partner. He was seeing a woman with many areas of compatibility. After a season of getting to know one another, he began to consider that she might be "the one". He began to organize and reason over the facts in order to decide if she was the one. Do you see the problem yet? Let me amplify. In order to assure himself that he was doing the right thing in asking her to marry him, he began to apply reason and logic. Specifically, he developed a formula for deducing whether or not his feelings for her were the kind of feelings that would merit a lifelong commitment.

Do you see it now? I am certain some of you still don't, while others saw it right away. I am certain of this because I know that we have different *ways* of knowing. So some of you are applying the same process as my friend did to these paragraphs, and you still don't see the problem. Again, different ways of knowing are intended for different circumstances. An academic way of knowing includes taking in data, putting it in categories and storing the data or bits of information. This is ideal for educational settings since most schools are looking for an infilling and recitation of information.

Another way of knowing necessitates activation. Picture a basketball coach sitting every day with his team in a classroom with notebooks and pencils. This would never be sufficient for learning the game. Basketball must be learned by playing. While understanding and knowledge of the game is essential, you cannot fully "understand" by information alone. Basketball must be experienced.

Falling in love is broadcasted and received on an entirely different set of channels from our previous two examples. Though it involves processing data and has an essential experiential component, it also involves the heart.

"Why is there a war against how we know and what we know? Because if our perceptions are distorted, then our desires can be swayed."

Love is an ongoing interchange of complex emotions and connections which are often very separate from logic and reason. To "know" about love through academic processes (logic, reason, and the collection of data) would leave out the most important processor in "knowing" love: the human heart. My friend was trying to detect an experience rooted in the human heart by a fierce application of the human mind. This is not uncommon, but it also is not effective. His *way of knowing* was incompatible with what he was trying to know, in this case, love.

A common source of human conflict, or at least significant misunderstanding, is to interact on a topic that requires one way of knowing using the processes of an entirely different way of knowing. In fact, this leads people to decide that their *way* of knowing must be superior to the other person's method. This ultimately prevents the resolution of the conflict.

This happens in marriages when one spouse says something like this: "Well, that is just not logical, so I will not listen to you any more." This also happens within cultures when one group says, "My faith trumps your science" or "My science trumps your faith." Is it possible that people are looking at the same reality through different *ways* of knowing? I have seen spouses do this more times than I can count. They remain divided to the degree that they refuse to even consider that another way of knowing exists.

This is why our first level of bondage is always bondage to definitions. Until we have a definition that suits the circumstance or a *way of knowing* that fits the target of knowing, we will remain stuck. Often, the first step in resolving marital conflict is to get the husband and wife to agree not on solutions, but on what the problem is.

Why is there a war against *how* we know and *what* we know? Because if our perceptions are distorted, then our desires can be swayed. If I can sway your desires, then I just might be able to use your will, your greatest strength, against you.

THE WILL

The human will is the flagship that carries the bulk of the firepower in this battle for freedom. By influencing Adam and Eve to use the force of their will, the serpent influenced the humans to give up their rightful position. Adam and Eve were not forced to abdicate their position, they gave it away by a choice of their will. Satan could not overpower them at that time. Like Judo, which utilizes the strength and size of opponents against themselves, Satan uses our greatest strength against us.

This is how the process worked with Eve in the Garden of Eden. She saw that the fruit of the Tree of the Knowledge of Good and Evil was desirable. Satan convinced her to disregard what she had been told, she took, she ate, and the rest is history. So the war to keep us enslaved is a war against accurate perception. If our enemy can keep us deceived, then he is able to use our greatest strength against us.

Let's illustrate this cycle of deception using our friend the acrobat. He perceives he is a farmer and a disappointment to his father. He desires release, freedom, but he chooses withdrawal and violence. He sees and experiences himself as a failure and a disappointment to everyone else. And the cycle goes around for a lifetime, wearing a deeper and deeper path in his heart. What would it take for him to be free? He used his will to become stuck, he needs to use his will to become free. But not simply by willing himself to act differently. As a young boy he turned his will against himself. Remember, when his mother and father became frightened and angry he had *decided* (an act of the will) that *being himself was too costly!* Though his circumstances prompted this shift, his will cemented it. He must somehow reverse this willful stance in order to be himself again.

A crafty enemy will know the most effective way to wage a war against us. If our knowing the truth makes us free, then our enemy can enslave us by distorting the content of our mind. He also wars against *how* we perceive the world around us and *what we do* with this input. It is difficult to know the truth if your *knower* is broken. Even learning about this war by reading information can give us the right information through the wrong *way* of knowing – a way that is incompatible with the practice of winning the war.

A parable can enable us to see an old truth through a new way of knowing. The parable of the acrobat can help us begin to see differently some things we may have already known. Let's see if the acrobat can help us again as we learn how to win the war we have entered.

Part Two

LIVE
DIFFERENTLY

CHAPTER 6

LIFE WITH THE ACROBATS

"I want to wake up kicking and screaming,
I want to know that my heart's still beating."
— Switchfoot, *Awakening*

I am told to just be myself, but as much
as I have practiced the impression,
I am still no good at it.
— Robert Brault

AT FIRST, it felt unnatural. Practices were difficult

and all of the apparatus were new to him. This did not feel like who he was at all. The initial excitement of discovering his identity had begun to bow to the daily tasks of learning this new life. The first time he touched the high bar it was almost electric. Now he often dreaded it.

He had been with the acrobats for a year now. His life was filled with new experiences, travel, and a constant flow of learning. He was building new relationships and growing into the routines of this troupe. Whereas the other acrobats his age had a lifetime of learning, he was just beginning. His true nature had been given no expression for the last eighteen years. Therefore, what was true about him seemed unnatural. This made the learning difficult and he often wondered if he could ever learn to be who he already was. However, he applied himself diligently to learning these new skills in the same way he had applied himself to learn farming. Learn the task, pay attention to details, focus on the work – this had pleased the man who had raised him. Surely this is what this new way of life demanded. He spent hours studying the various moves which composed the routines. It was exhausting, but he was going to get this right.

He was still getting to know his new father – his *real* father. It was difficult to relate with someone who was so completely different from the man who raised him. At every turn he was expecting the gruff, critical voice of the farmer. He had not heard it all year, but that fault-finding voice was so ingrained in his mind that he kept anticipating it. In fact, he was inclined to read criticism into his real father's comments, even though none was there.

Though he knew in his mind that this was his true family, his heart had not learned to connect this to how he saw himself. He did not realize how different from his true self he had become. He would eventually discover that some things he thought were true about him were not "him" at all. The more he got to know his true father, the more he learned about his true self.

"His true nature had been given no expression for the last eighteen years. Therefore, what was true about him seemed unnatural."

His first several months had been filled with discovery and excitement. Everything was new and exciting. No one expected him to participate in the shows, so he just enjoyed learning about the equipment and seeing what could be done with it. He did not start training right away, so he was in awe of the others who were equally in awe of him. He had become almost a mythical figure in his absence. Everyone had heard the story and some had memories of the days before his disappearance. In the minds of many, he had been elevated to something larger than reality. When he came limping back into their midst, the process of myth and reality coming together left many in the troupe with mixed reactions.

Most of the troupe simply rejoiced with his family at the return of the missing child. Some found themselves critical of his inability to live up to their expectations, especially as time went on. Still others, especially those close to his age, found themselves resenting the fact that he drew so much attention, yet appeared to have no skills whatsoever. Hadn't they worked hard for a lifetime and developed their skills accordingly?

The initial excitement awakened in him by coming back to his real family was now waning as the routines of this life took over. Every day he was challenged with the task of trying to transform possibilities into realities … and it was difficult. As unhappy as he had been working on the farm, at least it had been familiar. The memories and feelings of his former existence prevailed in his consciousness.

One of his favorite places to retreat was the quarters of the troupe historian. Here he could read the books and papers documenting the history and travels of this troupe. He found the commission for this troupe, signed by royalty from their home country. He also learned, for the first time, the nation of his origin. A variety of guidelines and by-laws were on record, all spelling out how the troupe was run – their organizational structure and accountability – and also how a variety of decisions were made.

Most interesting to the young man was the running travel log kept by the historian. It was like a diary of the troupe. He read the history of the people who had become his family and he knew that, somehow, he was connected to that history too. It was strangely fascinating to him that he had a history for which he had not been present. When the frustrations grew too much, he would retreat to this quiet place and read of the heritage he had not experienced.

Accusing Voices

The traveling and performing were intermingled with daily training and practice. The limp that had been a minor annoyance on the farm was a significant obstacle in this new life. While some young men his age accepted him immediately, others were jealous of this newcomer who seemed to have almost celebrity status among the adults. It was hard for them to understand why his lack of skills did not diminish the excitement felt by the adults as they brought him back into the family. Their own pathway to acceptance and approval was linked with their growing skills. For a few, their jealousy grew into rivalry. They constantly spoke critically of the newcomer, both in secret and increasingly to his face. This group would often conspire on ways to make practice difficult for the young man. If they managed to shame him in the eyes of the teachers, then that was even better.

Phrases like, "You don't belong here!" and "Why do you think you'll ever be able to do the things we do?" were aimed his way daily. These taunts stung even more because to him they seemed to be true. Particularly painful to him were the cruel reminders about his limp. How could he ever attain the level of skill that these lifelong acrobats had? Who was *he* to even be among them? What business did a cripple have among these skilled athletes? These accusations felt so true, in his own mind he agreed that his acceptance by the adults seemed misplaced.

These accusations also stirred up the anger that he had tried so hard to control among his peers in the farming community. In order to avoid fighting back then, he had isolated himself. But here, he was the center of attention! Whenever he felt the sting of shame rising, his temper would begin to rise along with it. His natural response was to return criticism for criticism and anger for anger. Though he was new to this life, instinctively he could recognize the weaknesses and faults of those who so willingly pointed out his. He remained outwardly silent, but the echo of their criticism grew louder inside him.

Strangely, this group of young critics also began to slander the young man's father. His position in the troupe had made way for this limping stranger to join them. In spite of the fact that he was a loved and revered elder, the younger group – which had not been around when his son was lost – began to allow their disdain for the son to influence their respect for the elder acrobat. Though the son never saw his mom and dad respond to others in a critical or unkind way, it seemed to him that, in general, this was how acrobats behaved. And wasn't he, after all, an acrobat?

Not only did he have a lifetime of training to catch up on, but now there was this war in his heart that seemed to sabotage his training. On many days he doubted that these acrobats were really his parents, because nothing he saw in himself would indicate that he was related to them. The accusing voices of his peers reverberated in his mind, even when they were not around. He thought about giving up on the training and going back to the farm. At least it was familiar.

a Father's Words

He spoke with his newfound father one day about these difficulties. He had hesitated to bring these things up, since his dad seemed so happy. He didn't want to bother him or let him down. It was easier to just smile and tell him everything was great.

When he slowly told his father he knew he could never develop the skills that the others seemed to have, he waited for the reply of disapproval that he had grown accustomed to on the farm. Disappointing the farmer had been a common occurrence and such let-downs were always followed by sharp words and heavy sighs.

This time the sharp words never came. Instead, his father's eyes welled with tears. "Son," he said, "we thought you were dead." Now the tears rolled down his father's face as he continued, "If you never learn the skills of the troupe, we are just overjoyed to have you with us."

"But Dad," he stammered, "you have been pushing me to work every day. Don't you want me to learn how to swing on the trapeze?"

"Of course, I want you to learn these things," his dad responded, "but it is not for me that I want this, it is for you!"

"What do you mean?" asked the young man.

"Son, the trapeze is *in* you, the high wire is *in* you," the father said. "If you learn these things you will be learning who you are. I want you to learn so you can become who you are, not so you can make me happy."

"But it's difficult and I don't know if I can ever catch up," he protested, hoping his father would be sympathetic.

"Son," the senior acrobat said, "certain things exist in your heart that you may never discover unless you push yourself hard enough to find them."

He heard the words and they even seemed sincere, but he was too accustomed to the treatment he had always received from the farmer. He had come to expect disapproval and disappointment, and he had convinced himself that his real father felt the same way. He misjudged his father's heart based on the content of his own. He finished the conversation with a mixture of relief and uncertainty. Surely his dad wanted him to improve his abilities? Surely his dad was angry and needed him to perform to ease his heartbreak? He was certain that someday his father would let him know how he *really felt*: just having him back home was not quite enough. He would need to prove his worth in this new life. He waited every day for this declaration to come.

"This picture of himself had become so ingrained that he had begun to consider the limp as part of his identity."

Yet, whenever he spoke to his dad face to face, he always walked away encouraged. His thoughts were increasingly clear and his confidence grew. His dad never wavered in his encouragement, support and love. It was in between these conversations that his practices and his peers would undermine his confidence. Every fall he took and every ensuing jeer made him doubt his father's love and the certainty of whether he belonged there.

Seeing Through new eyes

One Tuesday after practice he went to hide out in the historian's tent. He had been working his way through the travel logs. This day he came across something that first caught his eye and then captured his heart. As he read, his understanding deepened concerning that tragic day in the troupe's history. He read the record of the baby of promise. He came to understand the loving excitement the troupe felt in anticipation of the baby's arrival. As he read in black and white of the devastating loss, he could almost hear the sobs and strained conversations that took place among those he had come to know.

The hand-written pages reflected the pain of a tight-knit family who had suffered an unimaginable loss. The agony of the whole troupe had been recorded and it was right here in front of him. He saw through their eyes a part of his life he had only heard about. But something else grabbed him that day. He found *himself* in a story in which he had previously only seen others. Their history and his own intersected that day in his heart.

He read the lines again and again. Something was happening in his heart. He was beginning to see what he had not seen before. Just because he had not known these people or lived through their story, he had felt disconnected from it all. Today, as he read, he began to realize *they had known him.* They had lived through his story. He left the historian's quarters that day and everything looked different to him. Suddenly it looked like home. In the light of that experience, he began to see himself differently.

THE HEALING PROCESS

He spoke with his mother one day regarding the limp. It was during this conversation that he discovered another skill possessed by this troupe of acrobats. Because of the stress their bodies went through due to their lifestyle, they had learned how to take care of injuries. She reached for his leg and began to move it and twist it in strange ways. She pushed it to the point of pain and stretched tendons and muscles. Just when he thought he could not take the pain any more, she stopped. As the pain began to fade, he realized the dull ache which had always been a part of this injury had lessened significantly. He moved his lower leg and discovered some mobility had returned. It had improved.

Over the weeks that followed, his mother pushed his leg to painful extremes. As painful as these sessions were, the young man found that his leg was rapidly gaining strength and mobility. He could hardly believe that this pain and limp he had become so accustomed to might actually go away! He also began to realize how much he had thought of himself as one who limps. This picture of himself had become so ingrained that he had begun to consider the limp as part of his identity. The better his leg felt, the more he had to let go of something he hadn't realized he had embraced.

In many ways his practice became easier, but he discovered something strange. Now that his limp was diminishing, he still had a long way to go in his skill development. He had convinced himself that he could only achieve a certain level because of his impairment. As this became less of an obstacle, it also became less of an excuse. He now had to face personal limitations that had nothing to do with being "crippled". Now, when his peers pressed him for being behind in his skills, he could not point to his injury as a valid reason. This actually made some aspects of practice harder.

He still wrestled with the belief that he needed to learn acrobatic skills to find acceptance with the other kids and also to make his parents happy. This thing about becoming who he really was sounded good behind closed doors, but in workout sessions, or when he was tired, lonely or afraid, it did not bring relief.

One day, on his way back from a difficult workout, he walked by his parents' wagon and heard voices through the door. He had worked hard and he was tired. The kids had been particularly cruel that day. He fell, he slipped, and he simply did not perform well that day. On days like this, the urge to lash out and hurt someone was strong. He could feel the force of pain and anger surge through him, and the need to let it out was overwhelming. He wanted to hit someone. His shoulders slumped as he heard his parents' voices murmuring softly on the other side of the door.

"I feel like I am beginning to come alive again," he heard his mother say. "Each day I see him walk around the camp, I am so thankful that he is back with us!"

He lifted his head. This was not what he had expected to hear.

"I feel it too," his father said. "The ache we carried all those years is beginning to fade and is daily being replaced by joy."

"I see him try so hard and he thinks he is failing." Her voice was filled with compassion. "If only he knew what it does for me just to see his face, his tears, his laughter, even his frustration. All these things remind me that we have our son back. I am filled to overflowing just to have him with us again!"

He raced into where his parents were and looked his father directly in the eyes. Not only could he see the love and joy in his father's eyes, he saw something else. He saw something he had not seen before. As he looked into his father's face, he saw himself. He saw his own eyes, his own cheekbones. He was staring into his birthright and his heritage. In his fathers face, like in a mirror, he saw *himself*, but he saw himself in a whole new way. He was this man's son.

Tears filled his eyes and his throat felt thick. They really did not need him to perform in order to be pleased with him. They just wanted him back home. Being himself was really enough for them, without any change. In that moment, he began to remember something. He seemed to have made a habit of this forgetting process. He remembered again why he had decided to leave behind the life he knew. He did not leave because he wanted to work hard and be a disciplined acrobat. He did not leave to impress these other kids or his new parents. He did not leave to impress anyone. He left because of the fire that rose up inside him when he defied gravity. He left because of something in *him* not because of something in *someone else*. And he could feel that something stirring in him right now.

FOR an auDIENCE OF One

Tired as he was from the day's practice, he returned to the place where all the apparatus was set up. No one was around. They had all gone home tired, as he had. He stared at each piece of equipment. He now understood them much better than he had the first time he had seen them. He knew how they worked and how they were to be used. He knew the dangers associated with each piece and knew the possibilities for each as well. And in this moment he knew something else. *He knew he was an acrobat.* He knew real fulfillment was not in gaining skill or mastering these tools. He knew that the same fire that had drawn him back to this life was his and his alone, and that this was the place where he would find his life. He knew that no one could take this from him.

The same force which moments earlier had urged him to lash out, to harm someone, rose again … but it felt different. This time he saw the apparatus, not his peers, as the thing to conquer. His peers were not the enemy to be defeated. He believed he could take hold of these bars and make them his. The swelling energy inside him turned to focus on the equipment in front of him. Somehow, he was seeing everything differently … *everything!* It was not these *things* that had changed, instead it was as if he had put on glasses for the first time and he was learning what he had not seen before. He had changed his *way* of seeing.

Fatigue seemed to drain from his limbs as he approached the high bar. No one was there to scold him for climbing and no one was there to push him to work harder. He flexed his hands, hoisted himself up and launched. He felt like he was flying! Not just his body, his *heart* was soaring! He had gained some ability and the pain in his leg was less limiting than ever before. He flew … he leapt … he climbed and spun. He was driven by the sheer fun of it! He could go further, he could go faster, his adrenaline was pumping and he felt alive.

The sting of the farmer's voice, the jolt of the other kids' jealousies and the disappointment in his own soul – all of these things seemed smaller in this moment. The need to prove everyone wrong, as well as his own criticism of them – these were also melting away as he flew. All of his practice and study were helping him, but they were not what propelled him. Something inside, something infinitely true, lifted him up and moved every limb. This was not work, it was release!

He was discovering what his dad had said he would find when he pushed himself. He was finally breaking through the part that was "not-him" – the barrier wrapped around his true self. He did not know this logically. This is not the sort of thing that the mind knows. But his heart was more certain in that moment than it had ever been before. *This* is who he was!

CHAPTER 7

SHIFT

Neo: *"Why do my eyes hurt?"*
Morpheus: *"You've never used them."*
— The Matrix

"Open the eyes of our hearts…and let us see…"
— A prayer from Paul the Apostle

WHAT HAPPENED to the young

acrobat? This is the kind of question people ask, but it isn't always the most helpful question. We ask it because we think that if we know what happened, then we can reproduce the effect by knowing the answer. We ask it because we want "it" to happen to us also. But the answer to "*what happened?*" will only serve to frustrate us, since it carries no power to reproduce that experience in our own lives. Instead, the question we need to ask is, "*How* did it happen?" The opportunity for us to have a similar experience is embedded in the answer to that question.

What happened to the acrobat is clear. He became himself. He shifted from doing to being. He stepped into the life he was created for. He could have tried to become himself by controlling his anger and not getting into fights. He could have learned how to just cope with the heaviness that was so pervasive in his heart. He could have learned some strategies of self-talk to keep his emotions from running away and, therefore, stop the self-destructive behavior.

He could have done all these things and still not have been free. Freedom is when we can act and react in life as the person we were created to be. This can only happen when we have been restored to be able to live that way. The young acrobat's anger, the force of his emotions, the strength of his heart, all turned toward the intended goal: defying gravity. He did more than just stop feeling bad, he began to conquer the territory he was created to conquer – first his own heart and then the gravity which had limited him all his life.

How did this happen? That is the right question and now we will get the most helpful answer. How the change occurred is that he began to see differently. Remember, after identity, the next step in our formula is perception. We can change the target of our perceptual mechanisms and still see the same way. It is when we change *the way* we see that everything comes into focus. Now we can begin to know the truth and the truth that we know will make us free.

How it Happened

Here's how it happened. He stayed engaged, though at times he wanted to give up. He found himself in the story of the troupe, though he had no conscious memory of it, and even though he didn't feel like the new way of life was really his heritage, he decided to connect to it. He was willing to cut ties with his old heritage and all the ways in which it had defined him. He submitted to the healing process, though it was painful. He allowed his mother's skilled and loving hands to touch the wounded place, instead of shrinking back protectively from the discomfort. He didn't allow the voices set against him to stop him from pursuing his destiny. More and more he began to view things like an acrobat. Most important of all, he listened to the voice of his father.

What happened is that he came to know the truth and it made him free. I am not referring to "the truth" as merely the set of facts surrounding his real identity that he learned when he met the acrobats. Instead, he came to know "the truth" as he agreed with and embraced the right way of seeing himself and the reality around him. Too often we define truth as a collective set of accurate information or even doctrine. While the information or doctrine may be accurate (and therefore true), it does not necessarily have the inherent power to make us free. Truth is as much a way of knowing as it is what we know. Truth isn't the destination, but rather the compass that we travel with to get us there. Truth isn't subjective, it is grounded in the core of Someone … just as a plumb line is anchored by gravity in the core of the earth. When we compare other things to the plumb line, we can clearly see what is crooked and what is truly straight.

In fact, the way to know truth is to know the One who is the Source of Truth. Jesus said, "I AM the Way, the Truth, and the Life." Coming to know the truth is central to the war we are engaged in and we don't shrink back from pursuing it. But it is also surrendering to the viewpoint of One who is bigger, smarter, stronger and kinder than we, and who will do for us the things we cannot do for ourselves in this battle.

"Freedom is when we can act and react in life as the person we were created to be. This can only happen when we have been restored to be able to live that way."

OBSTACLES TO OUR WAYS OF KNOWING

Jesus and His followers have been around for years. So has the war against freedom. He faced the same war for His own ongoing freedom and the same obstacles. He set out to pass freedom on to the human race. It seems that most of the people of His day had the information they needed to know and understand the truth – it was what they did with that information that kept them stuck. In order to unlock all that Jesus gave us, I want to look at some *ways of knowing* that keep us from translating "true information" into real "truth" that can make us free. (Remember, we are learning how to think *differently*, not just different). All of these obstacles fall under the heading of *expectations*. Expectations are simply a pre-set mind. Like a contact lens that lays over our understanding, all input passes through our expectations. Let's refer back to our previous map:

(Identity → Perception → Desire → Choice → Action → Experience → Impact/Effect)

Expectations are wrapped up in our perceptions – of God, ourselves, others and the world in general. Our expectations are instrumental in shaping how we perceive things will be or ought to be. Expectations function both as a lens and a filter. Like contact lenses, we look *through* them but seldom look *at* them. Often that which does not fit our expectations is filtered out – not by conscious choice, but by our mind's failure to see what does not fit. We have a tendency to screen out what does not correlate with our expectations and perceptions.

Here is a great example. The religious leaders of Jesus' day were expecting the Messiah to be born as a king, and their expectations dictated that a king must be born in a palace and come from a well-known royal lineage. The announcement of the king's birth, therefore, would be clear and obvious to all. No one would have called these "expectations" – this was just how life worked. Therefore, the whole "manger, shepherd, unknown teenage girl" aspect of Jesus' story that we find so endearing worked like a filter over the eyes of the religious community. They weren't trying to ignore the birth of the Messiah, they just couldn't see it because they weren't expecting it to happen that way. Expectations can function as blinders or filters, or even act like a brick wall between us and the truth that makes us free. The following are a few categories of expectations that are particularly powerful in their subtlety.

Familiarity

The train tracks were less than half a mile away. On the north and the south of our neighborhood were major thoroughfares. This meant that the trains would sound their horn as they neared those intersections. When we first moved in, I thought it would keep me awake at night and drive me insane. Before we moved away six years later, I was sleeping like a baby and never noticed the trains unless someone pointed out the sound.

Jesus was known all around the nation of Israel for healing the sick and demonstrating the power of God, but when Jesus of Nazareth taught in His own home town, we read that there He could only perform a few healings and no miracles. God Himself was dwelling among humans! But they slept right through it for the same reason I learned to sleep through the sound of those trains: familiarity. "Oh yeah, that's Joseph and Mary's son … we watched him grow up." The filter of familiarity robbed them of the power of the moment and Jesus' neighbors missed the opportunity of a lifetime. Their God walked right by and they kept plowing their fields and tending their sheep. They never knew.

Familiarity is a filter we all wear in many arenas of our lives. We can walk by, ignore or take for granted the most significant people and moments of our lives. The words, "I love you" become a salutation instead of a passionate declaration. Driving a car becomes a chore instead of the adventure it was on the first day of drivers' education. Even though God has come to live in and among His people, we confine our contact with Him to a specific time frame on a particular day of the week. The habit itself numbs our sensitivity to His ongoing presence. Familiarity blinds us. Contrast this with the infant who takes in everything he sees, because he is seeing things for the first time.

By the time Jesus stepped into the human race, men and women were so familiar with the religious systems and laws of their day that they were sleepwalking through them. He had to start His first sermon by repeating the contrasting phrases, "You have heard it said … but I am saying to you …" over and over again. He needed to reawaken them to the fact that God was among His people. Familiarity with people, routines, relationships and religious systems can numb us all to sleep! The struggles of life act as a wake-up call sometimes.

Tradition

Tradition, the twin of familiarity, describes the habits and routines we develop as we respond repeatedly to what was once new. The experience of baking the first ever birthday cake for your one-year-old eventually gives way to, "Oh, I guess I need to bake a cake tomorrow" for your nineteen-year-old.

It's like the story of how a certain family always baked their Christmas ham. Mother and daughter were in the kitchen together and she pulled out a pan to cook the ham. The mother cut off the end of the ham, placed it in the pan and put it in the oven. A few holidays went by and the mother turned to the daughter one day and asked her to get the ham started. She directed her to get the large pan out, cut off the end, and put it in the oven. As the daughter sliced a chunk off the end of the ham as directed, she asked the question, "Mom, why do we cut the end off before we cook it?" Her mother replied, "I'm not really sure, that's just what my mother always did. That's how she taught me to cook ham." Realizing that neither of them could figure it out, they purposed to ask the grandmother, who was joining them for dinner.

"Our expectations are instrumental in shaping how we perceive things will be or ought to be … We have a tendency to screen out what does not correlate with our expectations and perceptions."

Later, as they all sat down at the table, the younger one asked, "Grandmother, why do we cut the end off the ham before we cook it?" The elder cook looked down at the ham, which was missing one end and a smile began to spread across her face. The smile turned to laughter before she could answer. Finally, she spoke. "Well, honey, the pan that I owned wasn't large enough to contain a whole ham. We cut the end off so the ham would fit in my smaller cookware!"

RIGIDITY

Familiarity becomes tradition and unbending tradition becomes rigidity. Rigidity refers to a way of viewing reality. It is a mindset that says, "We've always done it this way and change is evil." The reason for cutting the ham vanished with new cookware, but a rigid mindset refused to stop cutting the end off, even though the reason for doing so no longer existed.

Rigidity is a way of thinking that limits the fluidity of life and, in so doing, reduces the quality of life. The Pharisees believed that a crippled woman should stay crippled because people were not supposed to "work" (including healing) on the Sabbath. But Jesus healed her *on the Sabbath* because He had a bigger and better understanding about the true purpose of that day. Rigidity is not the same as order, though its proponents would say it is. It does not allow for change, growth, context, priority or any one of a multitude of factors that influence life.

Rigidity is often the precursor to collapse. In the building industry, architects and engineers have discovered that in order to build earthquake-proof buildings they must allow room for flex. When the ground moves, a building that is too rigid will topple. If the structure has some "give" to it, it will sway with the movement and remain standing and intact.

A woman sat in the chair across from me – back straight, shoulders back – studying this counselor before her, wondering if I could help. Her perfect posture reflected her training as a musician. She was the principal flautist in the local symphony orchestra. Her profession had nothing to do with why she came, but during our conversation she mentioned how much she despised music. She spent her days either teaching private lessons or practicing – something she had been doing for years. All day, every day it was nothing but scales, drills, exercises and more scales. This routine filled her days, but her life was empty. She hated what she did, though she was good at it. In fact, she was not just good at it, she was almost perfect, yet she was miserable. She had other dreams, other things in her mind that she did not have time for, but it brought a spark of life to her to think about them. Then she would sigh and put them away so she could get back to "real life": scales, scales and more scales.

I asked if she had *ever* loved music. She had not. It was merely her job. I asked if she had the freedom to improvise during her practice time, or if she could only play what was on the page in front of her. She looked at me as if I had asked if she liked fly-fishing – a look that combined "are you crazy?" with "why would I ever do that?" To her, improvising seemed like another form of what she hated already. Then I got it. It wasn't music she hated, it was *rigidity*. She was a technician, and a very good one at that. Every move, every note was in perfect control and there was no life in that for her. Rigidity will do that.

I enjoy playing the guitar. It seemed possible to me, therefore, that she had not experienced any of the positive things about music, since she hated it so much. Music has freedom and life and flow to it. She had not tasted that. All she knew was daily practice and technical performance. Eventually she quit the symphony and rigidity had claimed another victim. It had stolen from her life the life-giving experience music can provide. Approaching life from a place of rigidity will always suck the life out of life.

Expectations … familiarity … traditions … rigidity … these are strange but effective enemies of the life-giving experience of becoming yourself. Can you see how the acrobat became who he was really meant to be by overcoming these obstacles? He engaged purposefully in the war against them and stayed engaged, though it was far easier to give up. He didn't feel like this new way of doing things was his heritage, his tradition, but he decided to connect with it. He was willing to cut his ties with the past and all the ways in which it had defined him. He didn't allow anything to stop him from pursuing his destiny. More and more he began to view things like an acrobat.

Jesus came to set the captives free. The enemy of the human race has done all he can to war against this message of freedom. He has assaulted the way in which we think about Jesus. He has fought to confuse those who desire to follow Jesus, and he certainly has tried to distort the message of Jesus. Expectations, familiarity, tradition and rigidity serve as weapons in his arsenal to war against how we engage reality and how we digest this thing called truth. Yet, as the old hymn says, "His truth goes marching on". The truth is not changed by our confusion about it. In fact, the truth has the power to eventually break through our confusion, if we will stay engaged.

SHIFT TO THE One TARGET THAT MATTERS

Having looked at these obstacles it is now time to shift. The acrobat shifted. He laid hold of new things and he let go of old things. He learned a lot of truth in the process and he let go of a lot of lies. He fought a good fight and became himself.

At the center of the battle for my freedom and yours is a single target. This one thing has been opposed more than any other thing in the war against the human race. When this one issue is settled in your heart, once and for all, then all the other pieces begin to settle into place. If you have been around the church world, then you may have noticed that this truth has been opposed on multiple fronts. If you have not been circulating in that arena, the same battle has raged around you, but it looks different. Either way, I am convinced this one central truth is the beach-head from which the rest of the war is won. Are you ready? Here it is.

GOD IS WITH US

God is with us. He is here on earth. He is among the human race and He is ready and willing to act and to speak. He is present and He desires to interact with us. Somehow we consistently lose sight of this fact.

In the church world, battles are fought over many spiritual issues. These battles often begin with questions like, "Does God still heal today? ... What should a worship service look like? ... Should we raise our hands when we worship or should we be quiet and reverent?" These are debates which have split churches apart and populated new ones over the past few decades. But they all come down to the one fundamental issue: is God with us and does He want to interact with us, or is He far off, wanting us to get it right before He will engage with us?

"The presence of the Father, God, is the singular factor that allows us to reconnect with our true identity, to overcome the obstacles and to grow into who we really are."

If you are outside the church world, then the questions sound more like this: "What does church have to do with my life? ... Aren't all Christians hypocrites? ... Why are Christians so intolerant?" and so on. The question is not about denominational preferences, nor does it center on opinions about moral issues (though we have certainly made it look like that to the outside observer!) But the real question remains: "Is God with us or is He far away?"

Let's ask ourselves a related question: "Does the outcome of my life depend on my own efforts or on God's power working in me?" The young man in our story was an acrobat. He was born an acrobat and he would always be an acrobat, but when his destiny was hijacked, he lost himself. It is important to recognize that he would never have known who he was if his father had not come back to town. Equally, he could not have returned to experience his destiny if he did not return to life *with his father.* Instrumental in the young man becoming himself was the fact of him *being with his father.* In the same way, the presence of the Father, God, is the singular factor that allows us to reconnect with our true identity, to overcome the obstacles and to grow into who we really are. This is why it is so vital we understand that God is with us and wants to interact with us. Everything hinges on this truth.

Remember the Wind that entered the dead body and brought it to life? Imagine if this wind had hovered outside the room and required the dead body to rise on its own and enter the Wind. The body would have remained dead. But the Wind was *with* the man, and encapsulated in the very fact that the Wind came near was the power for transformation. The body was freed to be a living man.

When the father came to town, everything began to come into focus. The young man's old definition of freedom was no longer satisfying because he discovered the bigger picture of who he really was. When he decided to go with his father, he was freed from himself, or at least from the farmer he had become. When the young acrobat engaged his father in ongoing conversation, obstacles to freedom were revealed and progressively removed. Step by step, he became who he already was.

In the next two chapters I want to answer the question you might be asking: "What does all this have to do with my life?" Throw out what you have heard. The shift is coming. It's time to embrace a definition that can produce freedom. *Freedom is when you can act and react in life as the person you were created and have been restored to be.* Take this opportunity to have your own acrobat moment. Let the Father show you some obstacles, some false expectations, some things to let go of, and some things to embrace. Let Him heal you and begin to remove the obstacles that have kept you from being you.

Chapter 8

The Bible: God Speaks

"Twas brillig, and the slithy toves
Did gyre and gimble in the wabe:
All mimsy were the borogoves,
And the mome raths outgrabe."
— Lewis Carroll, *The Jabberwocky*

"But the words get in the way,
There's so much I want to say,
But it's locked deep inside ..."
— Gloria Estefan

GOD is with us. God is among His people. He wants to have a cup of coffee with you. He wants to drive to work with you, even when you don't want to drive to work. He wants to comfort you when you lose your favorite person, or any person for that matter. He doesn't just want to be involved in your circumstances, He wants to be engaged with your heart. The Father is with you at all times, no matter where you are or what you are doing, and He wants you to notice that He is there. More than just notice, He wants you to purposefully tune into His presence in these moments.

This most important truth is the central target of the war on truth: God is *with* us! All the filters we described in chapter seven try to prevent us from even noticing God, much less pursuing Him. We must push through the mental warfare and experience the truth that God is present among us. We need to view every situation through the perspective that He is more than willing to work in our present reality. When we take this high ground in the war, everything else will begin to shift and eventually fall into place.

God is with us. But how do we know that? How do we recognize God? Jesus said, "When you've seen Me, you've seen the Father." What does God want to say to us? Jesus said, "I only say the things I hear the Father saying." How does God act? Jesus said, "I only do what I see the Father doing." So what did

He do? Well, the first four books of the New Testament describe in detail what Jesus said and did during His time on Earth. But Acts 10:38 provides a good summary when it tells us that Jesus, full of God's Spirit, went around doing good to people and healing all those who were oppressed by the devil, because *God was with Him.* Jesus was the exact representation of God. By studying Him we can know what characterizes God and recognize His presence with us today. Even during those times when we don't *feel* like He is with us, we can be reassured that He is, because Jesus promised He would be with us always, even to the end of the world.

"If we learn to make the Kingdom of God our first pursuit, then our frustrations, our money, our pain, and even our freedom will be organized by God's power."

Jesus was very intentional about the message He came to deliver. Wherever He went, He talked about the Kingdom of God. He called it, "The good news of the Kingdom." Jesus didn't just talk *about* the Kingdom, He conveyed its truth through a variety of stories He told and He demonstrated the reality of it by healing people physically, mentally and emotionally, setting them free.

Seek First the Kingdom

Jesus made this all-important statement the first time He taught publicly: "Seek first the Kingdom of God and His righteousness, and all these things will be added to you." The "things" He referred to that would be added to our life were concerns such as our family, our finances, and all the details of our existence. In other words, these "things" will be taken care of if we seek first the Kingdom of God. Through our filters, we can read this as, "Try hard to do what God says and He will reward you with the things of life. Be good and your life will work out the way you want." This most common misconception of religion leads many to great disappointment, disillusionment and even resentment toward God. It even keeps many people away from Him.

We all have something we "seek first." It is the thing toward which most of our time, energy, attention and even resources are directed. Our degree of investment in it declares it to be the thing we value the highest. Whatever that thing is, it becomes what organizes every other facet of our life. If we seek first our marriage, then everything in life is ordered around our marriage. If we seek first financial gain, then everything in life is organized around money. Jesus was simply describing a principle of reality. Now watch: if I seek first relief from frustration, then I am giving the things that frustrate me the power to organize all other aspects of my life. If I seek first relief from pain, then pain becomes the organizing principle of my life. Don't blink here! If I seek first my freedom then my desire becomes the organizing factor in my life.

Jesus was saying that if we learn to make the Kingdom of God our first pursuit, then our frustrations, our money, our pain, and even our freedom will be organized by God's power, His provision, His wisdom, and His ability to affect any moment in time. Seeking first the meeting of your needs will ultimately put *you* at the center of your life – the very thing that got the human race in trouble in the first place. Jesus is encouraging you to make the One who is the Source of life your first priority. Then every aspect of your life will be empowered and organized by the Source who actually *gives* life. C. S. Lewis said it this way: "There are second things and there is a first thing. Pursue second things and you will have neither, but pursue the first thing and second things are thrown in for free."

Before we go any further, I'd like to restate these two vital points. First, the Kingdom of God is *the thing* that Jesus said to seek first – miss that and nothing else will work. Second, if God is among us (and He is), and He desires to communicate with us (and He does), then we must learn *how* He communicates with us.

THE BIBLE: a message FROM GOD

One of God's primary ways of communicating with us is through the Bible. It provides a lexicon to God's language. The Word of God is the vocabulary He uses to speak to us. The Bible is also the bestselling book of all time. That being the case, it follows that it is also the most discussed book of all time and, therefore, potentially the most misunderstood book of all time. I am certain that every possible *way of knowing* has been applied as human beings have tried to interpret the Bible. The filters that color our perceptions make it very easy to misunderstand God and our ways of knowing are often contrary to His. Getting to know God is simple, but frequently we make it hard. This doesn't mean that we are stuck, it just means we have to continue to shift.

I am not about to tell you that I have figured out what everyone else has missed and I am now going to enlighten you. However, I do want to tell you that the Bible exists for a specific reason and we can apply multiple *ways of knowing* as we read it. If we have misunderstood the reason for the existence of this amazing book, then we are very likely to apply incompatible ways of knowing as we try to understand it.

People read the Bible in a variety of ways: as a historical document, as a text book, as a rule book or a guide, as poetry, and some even read it to pass a class. Many read it believing they will get brownie points with God or religious leaders for doing so. There are countless other motives and filters that come to bear as humans read the Bible. I would like to suggest some helpful ways of reading the Bible, since the *way* you read will effect what you get from it.

FOOD

A certain woman I counseled struggled with compulsive eating. She wanted to lose weight. Needless to say, her body shape was symptomatic of the fact that she had learned to "seek first" weight loss. As a result, her relationship with food organized her life. Her daily routines revolved around trying to talk herself out of eating, but whenever she gave in to her cravings, she rationalized that if she walked a long way to get her food, then the exercise would cancel out the calories consumed.

She had a religious filter that suggested that God likes to make people jump through hoops before He accepts them. She had a hunger within her heart that she was attempting to satisfy with physical food. Knowing that kind of hunger could never be satisfied through eating, I suggested that she make some time to read the Bible during her day. Here is what I thought I said: "Make purposeful time for a conversation with Someone who cares for you, because He will soothe your heart and feed your *real* appetite." Unfortunately, she heard this instead: "Try harder to be a good Christian and maybe God will be appeased and bail you out."

She responded out of her own history, her picture of God, and her previous experience with Bible reading. "Well," she said, as she started to squirm, "I really don't have time in my day to do that."

I couldn't help but think about the conversation we had just had regarding how much of her day was spent in these rituals around eating. The real reason she didn't "have time" was because she thought I had suggested a dead religious ritual as a substitute for the thing she was driven to "seek first". I looked back at her and said, "I don't know if anyone has told you this (I held up my Bible), but there is real food in here." It could have sounded religious, or even corny. It seemed though, that this was one of those moments when God shows up to help your words have weight.

It was as though a fresh wind filled the room – I knew that from the look on her face. At first she looked startled, then confused. When the realization began to spread across her features, it was like watching someone wake up. Her eyes softened and then became moist. A single tear rolled down her left cheek as she spoke. "No one ever told me that," she said. She said it like she had been in the desert for days, her thirst becoming unbearable, and someone had just told her that water was within reach. How we view the Bible will dictate how we read it. I want to help whet your appetite for the food that can be found between the covers of this bestseller.

How Did We Get the Bible?

There are two ways I want to answer that question. The first answer deals with the practical, historical process of the development of this complex book. I will give the more expedient, condensed version of the first answer, just as a helpful background for the second answer, which will better suit our purpose.

Across the span of many centuries, God inspired people from diverse backgrounds to write components of what we now call the "Holy Bible". The first half, the Old Testament, was written by many different Hebrew leaders, kings and prophets. These documents contain various types of literature including history, law, poetry, instruction and prophecy.

Similarly, the second half of the Bible, the New Testament, is a collection of writings by a variety of people, each one inspired by God to write their part. The time frame for this section of the Bible begins with the birth of Jesus. The New Testament writers were Jews who had accepted Jesus as the Son of God and as their Messiah, prophesied in the Old Testament. However, these Jews were also writing to Gentiles. As a result, the New Testament documents were either written in Greek or translated into Greek from the original documents. The books of the New Testament were written to document historical events, or they were letters written to an individual or a group. The last book of the Bible is the book of Revelation – a prophetic vision of end-time events.

Eventually, the collection of writings we now call the Old and New Testaments were selected by orderly processes to be "canonized" i.e. included in the book we call the Holy Bible. Because this process involved a variety of people and groups, some Bibles contain writings that other Bibles do not. God used these processes of "inspiration" (God-empowered writing) and "canonization" (God-directed selection) to deliver His Word into our hands in the form of one singular book. Because the Bible was originally penned in Hebrew and Greek, the process of translation has also become an important part of making it available to the whole world. Since this process involves not just translating language, but also culture and meaning, today we have a variety of translations in many languages.

Sounds complicated? It is even more complicated than that! I have only given you a very condensed overview of how the Bible came into our hands. People debate every possible element of what I have just described and many more issues that I did not describe. Since debate is not our target, however, but freedom, I would like to give you another way to think about how the Bible got into our hands.

a Multimedia Campaign

The Bible must be considered as one part of a multimedia campaign designed to keep God connected with His people or, perhaps more accurately, to keep His people connected with Him. Remember, with each of us connected to God, the Source, life flows freely to us and through us. This is God's plan and it works better than anything we might come up with on our own.

God has never had any trouble expressing Himself, and to say that He is a really good communicator would be an understatement. An important part of good communication involves understanding your audience. When you understand their context and culture, then you can recognize how they think, what obstacles might prevent them from receiving your message, and even possible ways they could misunderstand your message. God knew that the very first obstacle to men hearing, understanding and therefore staying connected to Him would be our *ways* of hearing and knowing. The knowledge of good and evil is not a sufficient *way* to know a life-giving Father. It would be like trying to communicate deep passionate love through email. So God developed a multimedia approach to communicating with us, because He clearly understands our limitations. Here is a partial list of His strategies:

1. He wrote a massive parable – the story of the nation of Israel – and then played it out in front of the world.

2. The setting for this living parable is the Earth. Even the physical characteristics of the planet communicate truth about God's nature and His ways.

3. As the parable unfolded, He documented it through the writing of the participants.

4. Throughout the parable, He revealed himself personally to those who could then communicate to the masses.

5. He demonstrated His nature and power as He interacted with His people.

6. He sent angels and other visible representatives to communicate His unfolding script.

7. He found many direct and indirect ways to communicate that He would send someone to rescue those living out this parable, and the rest of the world as well.

8. He appointed many ceremonies and holidays to visually communicate His plan and His ways.

9. He spoke Himself into human form, becoming the man, Jesus, while retaining His divine nature. God the Son came to Earth while God the Father and God the Spirit remained in Heaven.

10. While on Earth, Jesus verbalized and demonstrated God's plan, His nature and His ways.

11. Jesus fulfilled all of the symbols and messages of the previous parable, simultaneously rescuing the human race from its fallen condition.

12. Jesus, doing what the Father desired, demonstrated how a human being can live by the power of God's Spirit.

13. God inspired witnesses to write down what they heard Jesus say and what they saw Him do, and preserved that written testimony throughout hundreds of years.

14. He sent His Spirit to live in and among human beings.

God reveals Himself in multiple ways, all of which can be cross-checked and confirmed by the Scriptures. When we understand how the Bible fits into God's larger plan to communicate with His people, then we can view it as more than a book containing history, rules or literature.

"You Think That ..."

Jesus spoke in pictures and parables (storytelling), visually and verbally. He spoke through actions and embraces. The message was transmitted through demonstrations of power and demonstrations of love. The message is also conveyed through the tugging in our heart to know Him better and to be transformed by Him. He not only communicated through language, but through every look, every wink and every nod. Every time we are weary, He supplies us with strength. When we are thirsty, He offers us living water. And in exchange for our pain, He has provided healing. These are some of the ways that He communicates Himself into our lives.

The scholars of His day, Bible scholars in fact, would challenge Him on whether or not He was "doing it right". Funny, isn't it? These scholars would point out sections of the Old Testament and try to "catch" Jesus being inconsistent with Scripture in His teaching or His behavior. Unlike them, however, Jesus knew *how* to understand the Bible. Listen to what He said:

"You search the Scriptures because you think that in them you have eternal life. And it is these that bear witness of Me; and you are unwilling to come to Me that you may have life." (John 5:39)

Jesus was saying to them, "The Bible is part of My campaign to get you to meet Me, to talk with Me, to connect to Me. If you think knowing the Bible is the same thing as knowing Me, then you will think you have found real life, yet be fooled. The Bible tells you *about* Me, but the purpose of reading it is to *engage* with Me."

Jesus taught through parables, but He also communicated through action because God is intent on engaging, not just educating. Let me give you an example of my own to help illustrate this.

a Schematic Diagram

As a musician, I have purchased several guitar amplifiers over the last three decades. The reason for buying the amplifiers is to help others hear the music expressed through me. Every amplifier I have purchased comes with a schematic diagram that looks something like the one pictured below, only usually much more complex. I want to ask you some questions about the diagram. First of all, is it accurate? If it is not accurate then the amplifier may not work. Is it actually a picture of my real amplifier? Is the diagram complete? Is every facet of the amplifier represented exactly where it belongs? If you are an electrician or an engineer, then this diagram probably makes perfect sense to you and you can see the absolute accuracy of it. But while the schematic gives you all the *information* you need to create this amplifier, it does not provide the *substance* – the wires, tubes or transistors – required to make it. In addition, an accurate understanding of this diagram will not directly result in making music. The accuracy and design of the amplifier are reflected in the schematic, but the diagram and the amplifier are not the same thing. If the diagram is wrong in any way, then any amplifier made according to the diagram will not work. Nevertheless, the "rightness" of the diagram is not the same thing as the reality of the amplifier, nor is it the true purpose of the schematic. The purpose is still to enable the guitar player's music to be heard. A completely accurate diagram, leading to a perfectly constructed amplifier, is still incomplete; it has not fulfilled its intended purpose until it enables music to be heard. We could debate this schematic diagram, study it, memorize it, or do whatever else we want with it. But unless we pick up an instrument, plug it in and play, we have completely missed the point of this complex schematic.

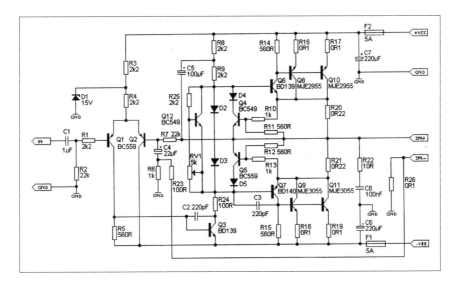

God designed reality to express the truth that is in Him. He then gave us a "schematic diagram" in the form of the Bible. Like the guitar schematic, the Bible is an accurate depiction of reality, but it is not the experience of reality itself. It is without mistake or error and is, indeed, consistent and complete in its depiction of reality. All of these ideas are debated in academic circles and the information gleaned from these discussions is interesting and helps us recognize that the Bible is breathed by God's Spirit and mistake-free. Yet, we can be in agreement with all of it and still fail to use God's written Word for its intended design.

The Bible is related to truth in this way: the purpose, or end result, of reading the book should be *an experience*. Specifically, its purpose is to help us know and hear God more clearly so that we can experience Him and then share our experience of Him with others. I encourage you to pick up the Bible, open it, and let God introduce Himself to you.

THIS IS GOD WE ARE TALKING ABOUT

I think it is crucial at this point to acknowledge what ought to be obvious. If the Bible is truly the result of God writing down His thoughts through men, then the Bible is significantly more than we think. It is so easy to think of God as being like us, because we are created in His image. We must remember, though, this does not mean that *He* is in *our* image – especially when it comes to our limitations. This is what I mean: the book you are now reading has been in my mind for a while. For years I have wanted to take the time to synthesize my thoughts and ideas and write them down. So you are now reading the "words of Bob". Just words … black ink … symbols on paper that your mind translates into meaning. But nothing is jumping off the page. Not so with God – just remember who He is! He is the same One who created the universe and the world we inhabit and His *words* were the building blocks He used to do it.

As a kid I used to dream about what would be the greatest super power to have. I know I am not alone – remember? Sitting around with your friends, trying to decide if you could have one and only one super power, what would it be? Being super strong sounded cool because of all the things you could do to show off. Then someone would mention invulnerability. Imagine if nothing could harm you – nice. Or, how about being able to become invisible? Oh, the possibilities for a pre-adolescent boy! Now that I am an adult, and can apply my superior logic (!) to this question, I think I have decided once and for all: I wish I could just say something and it would happen. I wish I could name something and it would become. In other words, I wish I could speak things into being. With this power at my disposal, every other power is just a word away. Need to be invisible? Just say it. What about super strong? Say the word. The Bible calls this ability "calling into existence things that are not …" and it is the super power that makes God, God. He is the beginning of all things, which means everything started with Him. If God wants to create something He is thinking about, He says it and "poof" there it is. Want a planet? Say the word. A solar system? No problem. What about a companion? Hmmm.

The most beautiful thing about this way of understanding God's communication is what this implies about our conversations with Him. We can merely tell Him ideas, but He can hand us stuff. We can tell Him about our anxiety, but He can say "peace" and in the word itself is the reality, the power, of actual peace.

He Said It

I sat across from a woman one day who was so overtaken by anxiety about the circumstances she faced that she was preparing to take her own life. She had formulated a plan and picked a time – all the signs that told me I should take her seriously. I gave her forty-five minutes of my best words. I counseled her like her life depended on it, because I knew it might. As I began to run out of things to say, I suggested to her that we might ask God what He would say. We prayed, "Lord, what would you like to say to this woman today?"

A moment passed by in silence, then she sighed, and then, strangely, she laughed – softly at first, but then her laughter became more pronounced. A bit worried, I asked her why she was laughing. She just continued to laugh. Her face was lighter, her eyes less burdened and the tightness in her jaw was gone. I asked her again, what had happened?

"If you are looking, listening or tuned in to the many ways God speaks, I believe you will find He is deeply invested in communicating with you."

She looked at me and said, "Well really, not much, I just heard the word 'Peace'." She went home that day to tackle her circumstances again, but this time with confidence and real peace. She decided to live. And she decided to trust that God would take care of her.

Now honestly, it bothered me a bit. I was almost certain I had said "peace" to her in my forty-five minutes of outstanding counseling. I think I had even said the word more than once. In fact, not only had I said "peace", I had also given her clever ways to practice it. The key difference is that the word of Bob is just a word. The word of God, however, is the same mechanism that He used to create the universe, and He still uses words to create today. The word of Bob *describes* peace, but the word of God delivers a package that contains actual peace.

The only problem with having this power is that your audience needs to understand, this is how you communicate. If they don't realize you can speak things into existence, then people will try to understand you on their own terms – expecting you to communicate like they do. As we get to know God, therefore, and learn how He communicates, we need to understand His methods of communication and the obstacles He deals with in trying to communicate with us.

Let me say here (lest you think I am advocating hearing voices) that when I refer to God communicating with us or "speaking" to us, I am not necessarily referring to an audible voice. God is Spirit and He speaks to our spirit. The wind inside of us (which I referred to in Chapter 3) is stirred when He speaks. People experience this in multiple ways.

Here is how I often refer to the way that God communicates with me: I have thoughts that are "smarter than me". Something "occurs to me" that changes the way I see or think about the matter at hand. It is usually not new information, but rather a shift in my perception of old information. Occasionally, I have a sense like the one you have when you feel impressed to call a friend and then discover that they needed to hear from you that day. Once I had the word "adultery" invade my mind as I was walking past a particular person. I later discovered that there was an extramarital affair affecting their marriage.

People describe many different experiences as "hearing" God speak to them. Most are not referring to sound waves, but rather to a stirring inside which is interpreted by their own consciousness. It has been my observation that often visual learners will see a picture in their mind. Auditory learners will have thoughts or words go through their mind and kinesthetic learners will get a "sense" as I mentioned earlier. I am convinced that God stirs our spirit through our connection to Him and we grow in our ability to receive and understand what He is "saying". The more we know Him and the more we know about Him, the more easily and accurately we recognize these experiences as ways that God speaks.

The Bible can help us interpret these experiences as well, since it records examples of many different ways that God communicates. Sometimes He communicates in dreams which are often symbolic, needing interpretation; sometimes He uses mental pictures; sometimes He sends angels as His messengers; sometimes He speaks through the words of other human beings; He has even communicated through a bush, a donkey, and a disembodied hand writing on a wall! There are multiple other ways that people in the Bible received communication from God. Some of them are listed in the "multimedia" strategy in this chapter. The others can all be found within the Bible itself.

"Spiritual things are not naturally comprehended. This does not mean that God is not logical. It simply means logic may not help us understand spiritual truth."

If you are looking, listening or tuned in to the many ways God speaks, I believe you will find He is deeply invested in communicating with you. If you are skeptical, analytical or looking for God to "prove Himself", then you may find that you are deeply invested in communicating to yourself. Or if you are angry, hurt or disappointed with God, then your heart might be resistant to receiving *any* communication from Him. You might even have difficulty believing that He *desires* to communicate with you.

a Periscope

Now let's look at a few other ways that we can understand and utilize the Bible, so it can become a source of food to us and not just another religious activity. In this book we have continually referred to *ways* of seeing and *ways* of knowing. When we, as residents of the natural world, begin to interact with the spiritual world, it follows that we will try to use natural ways of knowing (logic, reason, cognition) which are unlikely to help us access or understand spiritual ideas or realities. The *way* we see the grass, trees or mountains is unlikely to help us see God's work or purposes in our lives. The *way* we know or learn our jobs or our hobbies is unlikely to help us receive God's direction or input. Spiritual things are not naturally comprehended. This does not mean that God is not logical. It simply means logic may not help us understand spiritual truth.

The following chapters will help us explore the reality of the spiritual world that coexists in another dimension around us. Since this world cannot be seen with natural eyes, the Bible can help us begin to "see" what is happening around us beyond what we can apprehend with our natural senses. Jesus often used the phrase, "Those who have eyes to see, let them see …" He was letting his audience know that what He was saying to them had more meaning than their natural mind alone could receive.

The Bible can function for us like a periscope on a submarine. Just as those inside the sub under water can use the periscope to see the environment above the water, the Bible can give us a glimpse into the spiritual realm we cannot readily see. It can help inform our *way* of seeing. As the different writers of Scripture describe their experiences, and as we read different stories that demonstrate invisible realities, we can begin to tune in to a different realm, discovering what it's like and how it operates.

a Cell Phone

God desires to communicate and interact with us, therefore He must find a means to bridge the gap between His way of communicating and our ways of hearing and seeing. A simple and direct method for Him to do this is through written communication. The Bible can be understood both as an unfolding story, communicating His plan for mankind, and as a method of personal communication with each of us along the way while the broader story unfolds. This same book can be used as a checkpoint along our journey, to make sure that we are hearing His message accurately. As we read, different things will jump off the page to us and take on a life of their own in our hearts. The clever ways God uses an ancient collection of writings for immediate, specific communication is endless.

I awoke one night, startled, and I heard the word "Jeremiah" in my mind. My eyes were facing directly toward my digital clock and it read 3:33. The sense of urgency and the clarity of that word in my mind got me up out of bed. I knew that Jeremiah was a book in the Bible, so I looked up chapter 3 verse 33. Disappointed to discover there was no such verse, I started to go back to bed. However, I still felt pulled, so I looked again. This time I found that chapter 33 did exist and it had a verse 3. As I read, my heart jumped. *"Call to me, and I will answer you, and I will tell you great and mighty things which you do not know."* When I had gone to bed earlier that night, I had been asking God about this whole two-way communication thing. I had been calling out to God and He had answered. In the days ahead, God continued to reveal many new things I had not known before that night.

"Life-giving communication about the present can come to us as we read about the past."

Here's my personal favorite. I awoke early one Sunday morning. My house was quiet, which is unusual for a household of six, so I got up to have a cup of coffee and enjoy the stillness. I picked up my Bible and began to read. This was years later, but I still remembered God's clever Jeremiah moment with my digital clock, and I opened to that book again. Wondering about the context of the 33:3 passage, I backed up to Chapter 32 and began to read casually. I came to verse 38 which read, "And they shall be my people, and I will be their God." When my eyes finished those words, something sprang to life in my heart. Like the acrobat finding himself in the story, suddenly I had a deep and overwhelming sense of this verse and it was very *personalized*. I hadn't been looking for it and certainly wasn't expecting it, but casual reading gave way to deep emotion. I felt a warming presence right there in the room and felt stirred in my spirit as if God had looked me directly in the eyes and said, "You are my son and I am your Dad." That wasn't just a meaningful encounter for my day, but for my whole week! I was powerfully stirred and felt vitally connected to God and overwhelmed by His love that morning. Then I went to church. Worship was sweet because it felt so personal and I began to listen to the pastor speak.

To this day, I do not remember the topic, but I'll never forget the conclusion. The pastor spoke of God's affection for His people and, to underscore his point, he directed us to a phrase which is repeated again and again throughout the Old Testament. Before he even read it, I felt the lump in my throat, since I knew exactly where he was taking us. For the next two minutes he showed us reference after reference where God said to His people, "And they shall be my people, and I will be their God." I "heard" God saying again and again, "You are my son and I am your Dad." Though the encounter with God that morning had been meaningful, it was intensified as I realized that, days earlier, God had been preparing that encounter for me and many others, no doubt, during my pastor's study time.

Life-giving communication about the present can come to us as we read about the past. Direction for our own life can become clear as we read someone else's story. Assurance and hope can grow and increase as we see God dealing with families and even nations. The Bible can function like a cell phone, connecting us to God, if we will have ears to hear. So the Bible is at the language-level of God's communication. It is vitally important to us, but it points to a reality greater than itself. Just as the description of an experience is not the experience itself, the words about God are not the same as experiencing God. Someone telling you about their trip is not the same as being on the trip. The words about God have meaning, but should never become a substitute for the experience of God. Just what is it God is trying to get across to us? He is trying to get Truth to us, because He intends for us to be free, and He knows that truth – accurate perception – is the essential element of freedom.

As we said earlier, the first level of bondage we experience is to our bad definition or misunderstanding of freedom. Until we can understand what freedom truly is, we will try a number of faulty strategies to be free. Once we understand that freedom is about being who we were designed to be, we must have a way to know who we were designed to be. Once we understand who we were designed to be, we must understand God's plan to restore us to that state. Like the acrobat living life with his true father, God wants us to listen as He speaks truth back into our heart.

Chapter 9

The Gospel of the Kingdom

"Behold I am making all things new."
— Jesus of Nazareth

"The Matrix is everywhere. It is all around us. Even now, in this very room. You can see it when you look out your window or when you turn on your television. You can feel it when you go to work... when you go to church... when you pay your taxes. It is the world that has been pulled over your eyes to blind you from the truth."
— Morpheus, *The Matrix*

GOD is deeply invested in restoring things that have been lost. That is His nature. It can be seen in everything He does. The story of the Acrobat is the story of the Gospel, and the Gospel is a huge story – much bigger than just "setting you free" (although that is quite a significant chapter). The Gospel is the good news about God restoring all of creation to the "factory settings" – the way He originally designed it to function – and we get in on a good deal! To begin to understand the story, you have to start by thinking like a parent.

When we moved a few years ago, we were leaving the community where we had raised our family. I went on ahead to begin my new job and the rest of the family stayed behind while my wife, Jackee, wrapped up the details. She relayed this story to me. She had taken the kids on a tour of the homes where we had previously lived, pointing out to each child which ones they had occupied, as well as the homes where all their friends had lived around us. She decided to take them to the house where she and I had lived before any of them were born. When she pointed out our first home and explained that none of them had lived there, they all lost interest. Jackee and I can still remember our life before we had kids: things stayed clean, fewer things broke. We have many fond memories in that first home. However, as far as the kids were concerned, life began with them. Anything that occurred before that was the olden days and, therefore, not pertinent to their life.

Unfortunately, we adults sometimes think that way as well. We forget that God existed before us. It is difficult to imagine a creation without humans, especially without us individually! But rest assured, God was around before us and things were cleaner. We are messy kids and we break stuff. But if we can allow ourselves to think for a minute about life before humans, we may see parts of the story we would not see through our own eyes. Just as the acrobat discovered where he fit in when he read the bigger story of the troupe, we can also see where we fit in if we zoom out.

Consider the first ever committee meeting, the one where the plans were made for Creation. It was attended by the Executive Team of God the Father, God the Son and God the Holy Spirit. The three of them got together and the Father said, "Let's make creation." Now think with me for a minute. Where did that conversation take place? Can the question "where?" even apply when creation hasn't happened yet? I know this: wherever it was, God was in charge. The whole atmosphere of the place would have been filled with Him, His personality, His preferences and His power. It was a place that we could call the Kingdom of God. Whatever He liked or wanted was in that place.

"The Kingdom of God ... is a love and life-soaked realm, where everything works as it is designed and nothing is broken."

Our house flooded in 2002, but we had the good fortune of receiving an insurance settlement, allowing my wife to renovate the house from front to back. She chose the floors she loved. She chose the colors she loved. She even had some walls moved. By the time the renovation was complete, the whole house was a reflection of her tastes and preferences. It was the Kingdom of

Jackee (not to imply that I am not the man of the house. I just don't have preferences in décor!) It was her kingdom because her desires created the environment and filled the atmosphere.

In God's Kingdom, whatever is true about Him fills the atmosphere. So what would that be like? Here is what we know about Him ...

First, God is _love_. He is not just romantic or affectionate, God is the essence of love. I am referring to the kind of burning love that motivates someone to intensely pursue another with unwavering good will; the kind of love that will not tolerate harm or darkness; the kind of love demonstrated through Jesus when He healed the desperately sick. God's love will keep you from harm, even when you are the one causing harm to yourself.

Next, we see the truth that in Him is _life_. Remember the dead body that became a person? It is this quality in God that makes life happen; not just the absence of death, but the presence of "aliveness" in great measure. All life begins in connection with Him, the Source of aliveness.

What else is true about God? _Righteousness_ and _peace_. Righteousness does not mean the absence of bad behavior, it means rightly functioning, like a fine-tuned vehicle or a precision watch. Righteousness is a description of a perfectly fulfilled blueprint, where things are working just right. This is what permeated the atmosphere wherever that initial conference among the Trinity took place, before history began. The Kingdom of God is a realm in which the atmosphere always reflects everything true about Him.

The Kingdom of God then, is a love and life-soaked realm, where everything works as it is designed and nothing is broken. Anything inconsistent with this atmosphere would be automatically made right and filled with love and life, if it would simply enter this realm.

LIFE IN THE GARDEN

Having decided to begin this project called Creation, God began to speak the universe into existence. God created matter and brought it into order to demonstrate His nature, the way He likes things. He made the earth and populated it with animals. Then God set aside a plot of land, planted a beautiful garden and then He did something unique. He took something He had already made, the dust of the earth, fashioned it like Himself, and then

He put His *own* life into it. He connected this piece of creation to Himself. This being was not only like God, it was sustained by Him. Man was alive because he was connected to Life.

God had a particular place for the being He called "man". He named the man "Adam" and told him, "You manage creation and I'll take care of my Kingdom. As long as we stay connected, creation will look like my Kingdom." God's Spirit was connected to Adam's spirit, allowing God's nature to be expressed on the earth. The atmosphere of Earth was the same as the atmosphere of God's Kingdom. Adam lived immersed in love, life, rightness and peace. His body was never sick. God made a perfect wife for Adam and they loved each other with the selfless, generous love of God. Love was the atmosphere in which they lived.

There was something else true in that place, something difficult for us to understand. Adam and Eve could see things we cannot see with our physical eyes today. The Garden of Eden had trees with things on them like life and knowledge. We know what trees look like, but who among us has seen knowledge? Who knows what life looks like? Apparently they did, because they could see, touch and eat its fruit. Catch that! Things that are invisible to us were visible to them.

There was no confusion, no insecurity and no fear in Eden. Adam and Eve could respond to life completely as the man and woman they were created to be. They were free. They simply were exactly who they were, like a baby is before the realities of life begin to program its soul. As long as Adam stayed connected to the Source, to God Himself, he was in the Kingdom and the Kingdom was in him. Adam and Eve were fully alive and they could see both natural and spiritual reality. They knew the truth and the truth was keeping them free. Then they fell, not off a wagon, but from a connection. They unplugged from God's kingdom and the whole of creation plugged into another kingdom. They set an entirely different course for the whole human race, without even realizing what they had set in motion.

In the movie "Live Free or Die Hard" we see the bad guys trying to shut off the power grid that operates a large part of the country. In the scene where their plot begins to unfold, the camera pans back to a stratospheric view of the eastern half of the United States with electric lights illuminating the panorama. Then an explosion occurs and a spot of darkness appears. As lights go out in an ever-widening circle, darkness spreads like a stain from the center of the attack.

This is exactly what happened in the Garden of Eden. Into the light of God's Kingdom on earth, a spot of darkness appeared as man disconnected from his power Source. Within minutes, it spread to his marriage. The very next generation committed the world's first murder. Darkness spread from a man, to a marriage, to a family. From there, it spread throughout a community and infiltrated the culture. Soon, the face of the entire world was dominated by the kingdom of darkness.

Adam had surrendered his role in administrating God's Kingdom on earth to the deceiver, Satan, who began to establish his kingdom of darkness instead. From that moment on, God's arch-enemy began to destroy everything under his influence. Satan waged an all-out war to destroy what God values most: the spirits, souls and bodies of human beings, as well as the Earth He had made for them.

Let me assure you that I am not referring to Satan as some sort of euphemism for bad stuff in general. God is a Spirit who gives generously of all He has and He creates for the sheer joy of creating and sustaining life. Satan is a spirit who is God's opposite, He is not His *equal*, but His opposite and, therefore, he exists to steal, to kill and to destroy.

The course Adam and Eve set for mankind was more devastating than disobedience alone. They unplugged us from our Source of life and attached us to a new source: our own knowledge of good and evil. With *ourselves* as our source, we were left in charge of fixing our own problem; and all we knew to do was to hide what was wrong. The result of trying to hide emptiness is that it allows darkness within to grow, just like fungus grows on food that is hidden in the back of the refrigerator, out of sight. Adam and Eve traded the atmosphere of love, life and peace that they enjoyed through their connection with God for the atmosphere under Satan's rule: selfishness, death and fear. This was evidenced by the first marital conflict and the first murder. The whole atmosphere of creation changed and destruction began a steady march through all that God had made.

Finally, Adam and Eve had to leave Eden. Remember, Eden was more than a pretty place. In that place the first family could see things that were spiritual in nature. Because their disconnection caused them to lose their spiritual perception, those things became "invisible", imperceptible. Like a sound frequency that some can hear and others cannot, Adam and Eve could no longer receive God's spiritual frequency.

Satan got the keys and Adam and his wife got kicked out. I am certain that they didn't just leave the garden, but somehow the garden left them too. When mankind left the Garden of Eden, we lost more than our spiritual life and our homeland, we lost our way of being. We once had the advantage of perceiving things at a higher level than our five physical senses could grasp. It was as if we had more than just eyes in our heads, we had eyes in our hearts. The consequence of what Adam and Eve did was that the human heart became darkened and blinded, but it still yearned for life in the Garden.

Though mankind was evicted from God's Garden, we are aware that it still exists, somewhere. Whether it is called Eden, Utopia or Shangri-La, lost souls are still in search of God's garden. Songwriters and poets still describe the search:

"We are stardust ... we are golden ... and we've got to get ourselves back to the garden."—"Woodstock" by Joni Mitchell.

"God always had a plan to restore what was lost, and His Son, Jesus, at just the right moment, entered into the midst of the chaos and decay."

"Come into the garden ... pretend you're a child with nothing to hide, then we'll join hands and let the Universe swing wide—we'll lay our fears aside .... We've been sleeping all our lives, at last we can open our eyes. Our gates are unguarded. I've stolen the key to where everything holy inside us is free to run free—to smell and taste and touch and see"—*The Garden* by Carly Simon.

Notice that (apart from the Father's perspective) human nature automatically thinks: "We've got to *get ourselves* back to the garden", yet the path of self-reliance doesn't lead to the garden. Then we think we have to "steal the key" to enter the garden and enjoy our freedom. But Jesus said, *"I am the way, the truth, and the life:*

no one comes to the Father, but by Me" (John 14:6). We don't have to steal the keys to freedom, because Jesus has won them back for us. He doesn't just *have* the keys to freedom, He IS the key to freedom. It is no coincidence that the first place Jesus was seen after His resurrection was in the midst of a garden, beside His empty tomb.

If we lost the ability to see things that Adam and Eve could see, what else might we have lost the ability to perceive? The difficulty with a question like that is that if we have lost our perception, then we don't even have the ability to know what we can't perceive. The Bible tells us that a different dimension exists around us that we cannot perceive through our five human senses. But how can we know? Cut off from the Spirit, or Breath, that gives true life and spiritual perception, all that remains is the mind, will and emotions, and the body that contains them. Spiritually disconnected human beings are blinded to the spiritual realm and influenced by the god of this world – the one who thrives upon selfishness, death and destruction.

THERE'S a New SHERIFF In Town

Satan became the god of this world and he learned how to program the fallen human soul. His understanding of the roadmap of our soul enables him to take full advantage of our will, whenever it is not submitted to God. If he can succeed in influencing our perception then it sets off the following chain reaction:

(Identity → Perception → Desire → Choice → Action → Experience → Impact/Effect)

As generations went by, the decay continued. Eventually, people forgot that they were meant to live any other kind of life. They perceived reality merely through their knowledge of good and evil, so they remained disconnected and only knew God as someone to fear. Their limited knowledge led them to assume that God just wanted them to perform, to do good deeds. They had forgotten that He was their Father, that they were children of promise.

"What if Heaven is not a place for us to go someday, but a place which has come to us here and now?"

It is crucial to see just what was lost. Mankind lost more than just a secure spot in Heaven someday. We lost the ability to be the people we were created to be. Therefore, every passing generation grew further from the truth. Sickness was given free reign and selfishness became rampant. The accusing and terrorizing voices went unchecked. People's own choices and actions reflected and contributed to the programming of their souls, leading to their destruction. The world of Israel around the first-century A.D. was war-torn and the people were filled with every manifestation of the kingdom of darkness. The war against human freedom was in full swing and the enemy seemed to be having his way.

In spite of all this, God always had a plan to restore what was lost, and His Son, Jesus, at just the right moment, entered into the midst of the chaos and decay and said, "Repent, for the Kingdom of Heaven is at hand." What He did after that demonstrated that He had come to declare a war of His own. Centuries of living by the knowledge of good and evil made it easy for men and women to misunderstand Jesus' words. But one would have to be blind to misunderstand His mission. (Even if you *were* blind, He could help with that, too!)

Many felt that if Jesus was really the Son of God then He would demand that people stop misbehaving and clean up their act, before God came back to clean it up Himself. That whole idea is based firmly on the knowledge of good and evil. This is the declaration of self-reliance: that people behaving badly needed to behave well in order to serve God. But listen to the words of Jesus: "The Son of Man did not come to be served, but to serve and give His life as a ransom for many." This statement, coupled with Jesus' actions, made it clear that He did not come to demand subservience, but rather to accomplish for defeated mankind what they were unable to do for themselves. He began to exercise the power of life over death and sickness; He began to exercise the power of love over greed and selfishness; and He began to restore the minds, relationships, bodies, thoughts and perceptions that had decayed for generations. For Jesus also understood the roadmap of our soul. He knew that to tell people who were their own source to try harder just made the problem worse! People needed someone to undo everything that had been done at the fall. Jesus came to reclaim His sons and daughters and to begin to re-establish them in their souls and, therefore, in their experience as the children of promise. This empowered them to become God's representation on Earth.

Jesus very wisely declared first things first when He told us to "repent" so that we could receive the fulfilling kind of life He offered. Remember the definition of repentance? It literally means "to think differently", to change your *way of knowing*. The reason that men and women needed to see things differently was because their *perceptions* up until that day had made them slaves of the kingdom of darkness. Jesus came so that we could see and hear things from God's perspective. Until we use our mind in a new way, we will always view Jesus words and actions through the knowledge of good and evil, instead of with spiritual ears and eyes. After Jesus told us to repent, He essentially said, "Now look around with this new way of seeing, because there is a new sheriff in town."

So rather than think of Jesus describing Heaven as a destination we should strive to reach or as a location we may someday arrive at, what if instead, He was describing for us a place He had already been; a place that He had brought with Him to Earth; a place or a realm that contained everything we needed to turn things around. What if Heaven is not a place for us to go someday, but a place which has come to us here and now?

The rightful King has come to re-establish His rule, and under His rule men and women no longer have to be slaves to the destructive reign of darkness through their own deceived souls. The King has paid the price for our freedom. We are now free to become sons and daughters as we learn to see differently and enter into the Kingdom Jesus came to restore, but we have to put our trust in Someone we cannot see. We have to have, well, faith. We actually have to *live by* faith in order to enjoy the quality of life – Jesus called it "abundant life" – that He came to give us. Jesus came to exchange the condition of man – disconnection and spiritual blindness –

for the free gift of God: reconnection and spiritual sight ... LIFE! The gift of God would *have* to be free, since mankind had no currency to exchange for it. All they had was themselves and *they* were what needed restoring.

Jesus Was So nice

Let me be clear. I am in no way saying that Jesus did not ask people to change. I am afraid people have been very confused between Jesus' message and His character. People whose lives were disintegrating loved Jesus not because He was tolerant of their condition, but because He helped them get free from their condition. They loved Him because He was not put off by their need. He stepped right into it and demonstrated the Kingdom's answer to their need.

"True love would never leave someone trapped in bad behavior."

Jesus was nice, but He was not tolerant of harmful actions. True love would never leave someone trapped in bad behavior. Jesus was not put off by lepers or afraid to hang out with prostitutes; but He did not leave them in that condition. That would not have been the loving thing to do. No prostitute or sinner ever felt judged by Him because He was kind, gentle and non-religious. I am quite sure, however, that none of them thought He wanted them to stay in the condition in which He found them. He understood what held them in bondage, took dominion over it and then told them to go and sin no more.

The religious leaders (the keepers of the knowledge of good and evil) regularly tried to trap Jesus. One day they dragged a woman out into the square and threw her at Jesus' feet. She had been caught in the act of adultery and according to the Law, interpreted by the knowledge of good and evil, she should have been stoned to death. This meant that the crowd would throw rocks at her until she died from the trauma to her body. Those religious leaders wanted to see what Jesus would do. They demanded that Jesus judge the woman and render the verdict in her case. But they were totally caught off-guard by His response. Jesus saw things *differently* and His perspective on the case yielded an entirely different result than they expected. Jesus sized-up the situation and allowed a long silence to pass. The Bible says He stooped and wrote on the ground; no one really knows what He wrote. He looked at the woman and He looked at the crowd. Finally, He spoke: "Whichever one of you is without sin, throw the first stone."

One by one, the crowd dropped their instruments of death and walked away, hanging their heads. Jesus had successfully influenced the crowd to see things differently: from His perspective of love and mercy. Their self-righteous accusation wasn't a true reflection of who they were created to be. Jesus also knew that He came to pay the penalty for the woman's sin so that, on God's behalf He could declare her to be forgiven. Then Jesus turned to the woman to help her to "think differently" about herself:

"Where are your accusers?" He asked her.

"They are gone," she responded.

When you have been locked in a cycle of choices and actions, based on a perception which has been anchored in you by accusing voices, it is a great relief when they are gone! Jesus imparted His way of seeing, as well as the rule of His kingdom, into her heart. He destroyed the control the kingdom of darkness had over her life as he removed the blinders imposed upon her thinking by the accusations of the crowd.

"Neither do I accuse you," He said.

Amazing! The righteous Ruler of the Universe just looked at her unrighteousness and lifted the sentence. In that moment, Jesus changed her perception of God and, at the same time, her perception of herself. He did not crush her or expect her to clean up her act in order for Him to forgive her. Instead, He exchanged her condition for His free gift. The Kingdom power of love makes possible the Kingdom gift of righteousness.

But Jesus wasn't finished with her. He looked her in the eyes again and said, "Go and sin no more." He was loving and generous toward her, but would not tolerate the behavior which had harmed her in the first place, even though it had been her own choice. He changed the cycle of desire, choice, behavior and impact by changing her perception. Instead of thinking of herself as an adulteress – a sinner – she now knew she belonged to Jesus and was forgiven and free. In that moment, Jesus gave her a new identity. She saw herself in a new way: the way He had seen her when she first entered the square. The kingdom of darkness had lost another slave; the King of Heaven had restored another daughter.

WHAT IS THE KINGDOM OF GOD?

The Kingdom of God is the invisible but active reality of God's presence among the human race: righteousness, peace and joy. The good news of the Kingdom is that God has come to restore that which was lost in the very geography you occupy! He has not come to demand allegiance and enforce oppressive laws. Rather, He has come to repair the broken to allow them to "see" again so that, if they will, they might choose to return to the family and live life again as sons and daughters of the King.

The Kingdom of God is a spiritual Kingdom and therefore invisible to the human eye. It is a Kingdom whose atmosphere is love because Pure Love rules, not just as an attitude but as a conquering force. The atmosphere is righteousness, not because a rigid set of doctrines are adhered to by the force of will but because righteousness flows out of accurate perceptions. The atmosphere is life, not just as the opposite of death but as the force of aliveness that conquers not only death, but sickness, depression and every other thing that would try to drain the life from God's sons and daughters.

The good news of the Kingdom is a war cry against the rule of darkness on earth and Satan's temporary rule over the kingdoms of this world. Since Satan is "the accuser" his accusations directly assault our own minds and hearts and also harass us through the voices of other individuals in our lives, as we try to discover and become who we are created to be.

Passion: - financial stewardship
- teaching - communications
Kingdom economy, Law

The Kingdom of God is the presence and power of God to enable us to come to a new *way* of seeing and knowing reality, of seeing and knowing God. As a result, we can then begin to see and know ourselves more clearly as well. Those who will choose to see differently, through God's perspective, will be free to exercise their will to be who they truly are, not who they had become.

THE KINGDOM OF GOD IS LIKE A RADIO STATION

In order to help us sense more of what Jesus was saying, I would like to submit a modern day parable. Jesus told us to repent or, as we have said, change the way we perceive the world. He told us to do so because we coexist in this world with an invisible Kingdom. It cannot be perceived in the ways the earthly realm is perceived, nor can its power be accessed the way we access human power. This is hard for our rational minds to wrap around, so let's consider an illustration we all understand.

The Kingdom of God can be compared to a radio station. Unless you are out in the wilderness right now, the air around you is completely saturated with radio waves. They pass over and around you, as well as through you. You cannot touch, taste, smell, hear or see them. But if you have lived in modern society, you know they are present. It takes little or no faith to believe in the presence of radio waves, because we have so much experience with them. Even if we don't understand how they work, we know that they do work. We understand the fact that we do not hear the signal being broadcast by the radio station if we have no receiver, or if our receiver is not plugged in, turned on and tuned to the frequency. The antenna draws in the signal from the air waves. The guts of the receiver turn the signal into words or music and then the amplifier and speaker broadcast the sound.

In the same way the Kingdom is all around us. The presence and power of God is among us, passing through and over us. The atmosphere around us is saturated with God. Yet, without a receiver present, life goes on as usual. Sickness, sorrow and darkness seem to be unaffected. Our dilemma is that many receivers are present, but few are plugged in; the ones that are plugged in are not turned on or tuned in to His frequency.

We humans are designed to be receivers of the Kingdom. "Let us make man in our own image" is not just a declaration of visual similarity. Just like

God, we are made in three parts: spirit, soul and body (we'll be looking at this more closely in the next chapter). In fact, originally we contained the very Spirit of God. It was Adam and Eve that unplugged us all. When they were banished from the Garden, they were disconnected and lost the signal. The new birth, which Jesus talked about, is what reconnects us to God, our Power Source. Jesus told Nicodemus, "Unless a man be born again, he cannot *see* the Kingdom of Heaven." We are not able to receive until we get plugged back in. Unfortunately, many are plugged back in, but fail to locate the "on" switch, or are never taught to "tune in" to God's frequency. If we are ever going to broadcast the Kingdom, we must be born from Heaven, we must be paying attention to Heaven (seeking first the Kingdom) and we must be tuned in to Heaven's signal – the Voice of the Broadcaster.

THE KINGDOM OF GOD IS LIKE an Oven

We have described the Kingdom as the presence and the power of God. The Kingdom is a concept defining God's work, not the work of humans. So what about humans? Don't we have some role in this relationship with God thing? Absolutely we do! So to help us further, consider this parable: The Kingdom of God is like an oven.

The oven is an environment of intense heat. Anything placed within the oven is changed by the heat. Cookie dough exerts no effort of its own to change itself, it must simply enter the oven. The heat will do what it does. Heat causes ice to become water, water to become steam, and batter to become brownies.

The atmosphere of the Kingdom, just like an oven, has a transforming power all of its own. As we have said previously, that power is life, love, peace, joy and rightness. If you dive in, then these forces will begin to change you. Try to live on your own resources and these powers will have no effect on you. The Kingdom of God has the power to effect anything that enters its atmosphere. Our role? Enter in; change our source; surrender self-reliance and surrender to the immediate present rule of God. He will bake you. Change will come, but it will be His power, not your effort, that changes you.

WHY ISN'T EVERYTHING BETTER NOW?

The question always arises: "If Jesus brought the Kingdom of Heaven and the Kingdom of Heaven makes things right, why are so many things still not right? Since the King has returned and taken dominion over all the authority of the previous ruler, why does sickness still happen and why does darkness still hang on? It is an important question, because it helps us define and understand the times we live in and the nature of the battle still at hand. And it helps us to partner with God as we answer that question.

Jesus has turned the reigns back over to us. He has reissued God's assignment to Adam and Eve: take dominion. We are living in the age when it is our assignment to regain what we lost. Our next chapter, "Freedom from Obstacles", will show us where we are in the war, as well as helping us to further understand the nature of the battle. If your eyes have been opened to the bondage of your old definitions, then you have come to new ways of seeing and knowing. If you have gotten this far, you can become free from yourself, as you see the trap inherent in your humanity and the disconnected life. In this next chapter, I want to give you a roadmap of the kinds of obstacles that we face. I want to help you see how our Father in Heaven comes near to rescue us and is still the one who overcomes these obstacles for us.

CHAPTER 10

FREEDOM FROM OBSTACLES

"Freedom is what you do with what's been done to you."
— Jean-Paul Sartre

"I want to run, I want to hide,
I want to tear down these walls that hold me inside ..."
— U2, Where the Streets Have no Name

SHE LOOKED over the top of her thick-rimmed glasses like a child looks around the skirt of their protective parent. The interview had gone well, up until that moment, for this well-dressed professional woman. She had all the experience and qualifications we were looking for, but she had thirty years of terror just below the surface of her words.

"What do you think about me?" she asked. Her voice contained a mixture of protective defiance and stark uncertainty. She had asked the question we all are asking.

She had served us the package. She handed over everything she had learned in her work and everything she knew about herself, and now her face and her question revealed the absolute vulnerability she felt, having placed herself in our hands. This was my first encounter in what has turned out to be a longstanding working relationship and a growing friendship. We hired her later that week and began a journey together to answer not only the question she asked, but also the unspoken question underneath it: "What did she think of herself?"

In the months and years ahead, I saw that look again and again. Sandy would offer her thoughts and opinions and then physically withdraw, looking out from behind eyes that measured the response to her exposure. She would lean in and lean out with palpable fear. Sometimes she seemed like a hard-edged taskmaster, other times like an anxious schoolgirl.

As time went on, I grew certain that below this outward tentative presentation swirled a deep pool of strength, wisdom and compassion. Some days I could see those qualities with clarity, then other days they seemed so hidden behind her dance that I wondered if I had really correctly identified her gifting. She interacted haltingly with others, still asking the question, "What do you think about me?" whether with words or actions. One day I watched her completely freeze, paralyzed by her anxiety, as she spoke to a group of about forty co-workers. As time went on, familiarity and constancy brought down a few of the walls, but overall she had remained armor-clad, wrapped in a hard shell of fear. I had grown accustomed to the dance and did my best to keep from fulfilling her negative expectations. In a moment, one spring day, everything changed.

"The pain of those vicious words and actions, the tormenting voices she heard in her thoughts, and the instinctive self-protection that grew out of that terrible year – all those things combined to create a false picture in her own heart of who she really was and how others viewed her."

We train people in helping others be healed and set free. An essential piece of this training includes hands-on exercises, providing the opportunity to be released from your own traps. It was on one of these training days that the armor broke and fell away. After the break time, Sandy came back to the room full of trainees, her face glowing and tears streaming from her once fearful eyes. Without the customary hesitation, she spoke easily and powerfully to a room full of forty co-workers.

"I've been healed," she said, weeping.

Those three words turned every head in the room. More than the meaning of the words, it was the weight and the gentle power behind them that turned our heads and moved our hearts. It was the stark exposure of this gentle soul (unguarded, for a change) that caught our attention in that moment. She sounded different and she looked different. This beautiful woman who had frozen in fear every time she was asked to speak in front of people, and had been gripped with anxiety any time she spoke even one-on-one with me, began to unfold her story. It was a story that had us all in its grip. Those of us in that room were compelled not just by the story, but also by our personal experience with Sandy's fears which, in that moment, were nowhere to be found! Like the blind man who looked others in the eyes while he talked of Jesus healing him, this once fear-bound woman looked confidently into the eyes of a roomful of people and declared she was no longer afraid.

This African-American woman had grown up in the same culture that we all had. However, we had not experienced the level of accusation and abuse that she had suffered at the hands of prejudiced white educators. Sandy began to tell us of the white male teacher who had regularly informed both her and the rest of the class that she was stupid. He had consistently subjected her to verbal shame and even injustice. She was falsely accused and publicly punished for the wrongdoing of one of her classmates – a white girl. The evil committed against her during that school year culminated one day with the same teacher humiliating her in front of the class by locking her in a closet. As outrageous as this was, he apparently forgot he had left her in the closet and she was not found until later when her family began to look for her that evening.

Emotionally shut down? She was far more than shut down! The pain of those vicious words and actions, the tormenting voices she heard in her thoughts, and the instinctive self-protection that grew out of that terrible year – all those things combined to create a false picture in her own heart of who she really was and how others viewed her. Her memory had linked me with that teacher she had feared, since I was another white male authority figure in her life. In a moment, the looks, the fear, the dance of the previous years all made sense. No matter how well I actually treated her, someone else had already programmed her with how this would play out. But that day her programming changed in a moment.

We all listened intently as Sandy continued her story with what happened that wonderful moment to cause the fear to leave her. She had been partnered with one of our other team members and they asked God about her past and the lies she might have believed. In that moment, God brought to her mind specific memories of those unbelievably painful and shaming events. He showed her that, because of those events, she had believed lies about Him, about herself, and about how other people saw her. She had believed the lie that she was stupid and that no one really valued her contribution. She had believed that God had abandoned her and would not watch out for her. She had believed that everyone around her saw her this way, so she lived in constant expectation of shame and humiliation, especially from her white male boss.

"When we discover that He made us to be much more than we ever dreamed ... We will experience life!"

This time when she saw those painful memories in her mind, she saw them through different eyes. She saw that God had been there for her in those moments, and she saw herself not through the eyes of that teacher, but through the eyes of her loving Father. She said she felt something warm begin to spread over her body, starting at the top of her head and covering her from head to toe. As it did, she felt a physical sensation of the fear leaving her. A week later, Sandy stood in front of two hundred and fifty co-workers and told the story again with a strong, steady and unguarded heart – and with no trace of fear or shame. She freely shed her tears and spoke with certainty that the perfect love she had been covered with that day had actually washed the fear out of her.

She has never been the same since. The harassing voices she once heard constantly (and thought she deserved) are gone. I no longer see any hardness in her eyes. The fear has been replaced by light and joy. Today, three years later, she laughs easily. Her countenance is soft and her smile is spontaneous and warm. The once scared child is now playful, enjoying the interaction with her co-workers. Whether in the thick of crisis or over a relaxed lunch, Sandy has become herself, and she doesn't look anything like the woman I used to know.

This is freedom, and this is what God has made available to us all. When we discover that He made us to be much more than we ever dreamed – and if we'll allow Him to show us the obstacles in the way – then we will experience much more than just the absence of those obstacles. We will experience life!

Obstacles

So what kinds of obstacles block our freedom? Even at this stage, our definitions matter. The obstacles are never our circumstances; they are not around us, but within us. Victor Frankl, author of the book *Man's Search for Meaning*, demonstrated how even the residents of the death camps of World War Two had the opportunity to be free. They were free to choose to be themselves, regardless of circumstance or how they were treated. That is the mark of true freedom.

In this chapter we will examine two categories of obstacles: the natural and the spiritual. I wish those distinctions were really as clear as they sound. The overlap between the two, centers around how life has programmed our souls and, as a result, how we understand and interact with the world around us – both the natural and spiritual world. Let's use one more parable to help us see.

Natural Obstacles

Humansysco is a company that creates products and services to make a better society. Under the leadership of the founder and CEO, the business grew from the ground up into a cutting-edge organization. He had a unique ability to guide such a complex machine with its many departments, each with its own structure and processes. The CEO also developed a unique system of communication, allowing all that diversity to function in perfect symphony under his strong leadership. But upon his departure, the company began to disintegrate. Without his guiding hand and his unique strategy for connectivity, the complexity of the organization began to work against itself.

The Operations Department was created to make and implement the decisions that sustained productivity. Under the founder's guidance, this department could produce amazing results and served as the major catalyst to effect great change. However, it needed the input and support of the next two departments.

Information Systems was designed by the founder to be the hub of communication. They existed to collect, store, integrate and disseminate data. Customer feedback, market fluctuations, cash flow – you name it – both internal and external sources of information flowed through this department. It was their job to examine and determine who needed what information and then get it into the hands of the right department. Information Systems was designed by the Founder to function in a sort of checks-and-balances relationship with the next department.

Mind

Internal Affairs was designed to monitor and strengthen the organization by keeping everyone connected to and celebrating the victories of the company. Their job was to monitor the experiences of the employees and to make sure that any individual victory was also experienced as a corporate victory. Internal Affairs communicated any and all good news throughout the company and processed things from a different perspective than Information Systems.

The Security Division was a later addition to the company. The need for it emerged after the departure of the Founder, when the company became less integrated without his guiding influence. Initially, it seemed important to be sure that each department had back-up when dealing with external businesses and agencies. But as time went on, it was ironic how this department's response to the need for safety and security became more of a problem than a solution.

It took very little time to recognize how important the unifying leadership of the Founder had been in maintaining the company's increasing size and influence. Following his departure, many tried to maintain the internal connectivity their leader had fostered. However, without the centralized authority, problems and disagreements were inevitable. As new employees came in, who had not been under the Founder's leadership, they assumed the chaos and confusion were normal.

The departments that had once worked in unison now found themselves divided and even worse, sometimes in competition. Information Systems, once the support of Operations, began to consider themselves more knowledgeable than the other groups. As a result, they tried to take authority that belonged to other departments. Because they had the ability to get things done, Operations often tried to override or even undermine the other departments. And Internal Affairs, designed to maintain company morale, began to take sides in conflicts, forming alliances and furthering the very strife they were trying to resolve. Security became an enforcer in these internal conflicts and would also take sides based on circumstances. Every internal conflict was magnified and it seemed this once flourishing company was destined for failure. Without any kind of unified headship, no single department, or even alliance of departments, had the ability to rescue the sinking ship. In fact, their efforts only seemed to make things worse.

Each of the departmental systems in our story represents an aspect of the human soul and how our soul can actually become divided and work against itself. The disintegration of Humansysco is a picture of how our soul malfunctions when our spiritual nature isn't connected to God, our Founder and CEO.

Internal Agreement

The problems encountered in this company all have one overriding theme: there is no internal unity and agreement. If you have ever said or thought, "I know this is true in my mind, but it just feels like it is not true." Or if you have asked yourself the question: "Why is it I keep doing this thing that I really do not want to do?" then you are describing the condition of internal disagreement.

We have a mind, not just a brain. Like the *Information Systems Department*, our brain gathers data from our five senses, records it, retrieves it and sends impulses to our body accordingly. Our *brain* is the physical organ that our mind uses. Our *mind*, however, is more than just a container of programmed thoughts. Our mind interprets our thoughts, evaluates them, makes plans, etc. This is the part of ourselves that we are most aware of because we are thinking all day long. We also make observations and then reason out their meaning.

> *"What we believe in our heart, whether true or false, is what we become ... He designed our mind to consult with our heart – a heart yielded to His Spirit living within us – so we would stay on the right course."*

We have feelings and experience a range of emotions (whether we think we do or not, and even if we are not comfortable with them ... we DO have feelings). This is how we experience "being ourselves" in any given moment or situation. It feels good, or bad, to be *you* right now. As our mind processes, our emotions respond. Our thoughts have the power to instigate and even inflame our feelings, but conversely our feelings have the power to reveal what we really believe about a given situation or person. The Christian world has been told for years that their feelings will deceive them. People who are afraid of their emotions can use this idea to distance themselves from feelings that are uncomfortable. I would like to go on record at this point to dispute this dangerous idea that our feelings will deceive us. I am convinced that our feelings will *always tell us the truth*: not necessarily the truth about reality, but the truth about *what we believe*. Our feelings come from the heart, which is where belief is generated (obviously I am not referring to the organ that pumps our blood, but rather the part of us that contains our deepest convictions and beliefs that reveal who we are). The Bible tells us, "As a man thinks in his heart, so is he." What we believe in our heart, whether true or false, is what we become. Our heart doesn't just house our feelings but also our conscience. In fact, just as the *Internal Affairs Department* in our fictitious company was designed to monitor and strengthen the entire organization, keeping it tuned in to victory, our heart was designed by God to serve as the monitor and interpreter between our spirit and our mind. He designed our mind to consult with our heart – a heart yielded to His Spirit living within us – so we would stay on the right course.

We also have a will, a decider. This coincides with the *Operations Department*. It is the part of us that initiates action or restrains action. It is the steering mechanism of our soul. Our decider takes in the data from our mind, considers our feelings, and makes a choice based on weighing out the data from both. If we seek first something from the mind or the feelings, then we have put a *part* of us in charge of the rest of us, and the wrestling match begins!

These three, the mind, the emotions and the will, combine to make our soul, the self, the part of us that rides around in our body. This is what makes us uniquely "us" and unlike anyone else. Personality is the image our soul projects to others, and the strengths and weaknesses in our soul define our character. Our mind, will and emotions develop the roadmap we use regarding perception, desire, choice, action, experience and impact. This is where the battle takes place and the offensive strategy the enemy uses against us is called "divide and conquer". What keeps us from being divided, what keeps us connected and balanced, is the Spirit, or Breath, of the One who made us. This is the part that changed when Adam and Eve messed up. It is important to know that they did not eat an apple, as many think. The fruit of the Tree of the Knowledge of Good and Evil was a very specific fruit they ate that day and it had a very specific impact.

Returning to our Humansysco illustration, when we disconnect from God, our CEO, then a new "department" tends to emerge. Remember the *Security Division?* It developed in response to the need we humans have for safety and security, but it caused more problems than it solved. Whenever we look to ourselves to meet those needs, instead of God, then we adopt the fear-driven strategy of self-protection. Some people even become paranoid. They rely upon their knowledge of good and evil, causing them to see enemies where there aren't any – as was the case with Sandy. Her painful past had trained her to "protect" herself from what she imagined would happen.

The other component that we need to understand is our flesh: the physically driven part of us. The flesh includes all the systems of the body, including the physical structures of the brain, the heart and the nervous system that process the various elements I just described as your soul (the mind, will and emotions). Your nervous system continually feeds you information about yourself. Because of the interaction of all these parts, we are highly programmable creatures. We can learn in more than one way, as we have discussed. We can also have internal disagreement within ourselves. We can know things with our mind that our emotions disagree with. Our flesh can also store data contrary to our feelings.

Congruence

An important part of becoming who we are created to be is congruence, or integration, of all these components. It is the role of God's Spirit in us to bring all of these facets of our self into unity. When we are our own source (as is the case before we reconnect to God), the likelihood of conflict among these components is high. Even after we are reborn, if we do not understand that it is the Spirit's job to bring truth to our soul, then we can remain or become even more conflicted.

Let's look at our acrobat again. Separated from his parents, he began to live outwardly a life that was different from his inner design. The war between his mind and his emotions raged every day. The day his mother found him climbing and his dad became angry, his will turned against his mind and emotions. Remember, he decided in his heart to never frighten her again, which meant part of him decided not to be him. The will is a powerful force, so his own strength was working against him. His heart still stirred with the hidden truth about himself, but his emotions and mind, coupled with the force of his will, actually prevented him from being who he really was.

What about the woman who had her first menstrual cycle in her thirties? Her body joined in the war within her soul. Some people try to change their behavior while their souls are still at war, but they have little chance of changing outward performance when their inner life is in so much turmoil. Let's take a look at a few key obstacles commonly encountered in the battleground of our soul.

You can't handle responsibility and you should worry about the outcomes of tomorrow.

CORE LIES

"Women are weak and women are victims, and I will not be one." She had been locked in and locked down by these words before she ever spoke them. We called it "The Big Lie". We have defined truth as more than just accurate facts. In the same way, a core lie is more than just *inaccurate* facts. For the acrobat, the core lies were: "You are a farmer" and "You are bad when you follow your heart".

Core lies are the ones that attack or undermine our identity and any attempt to be that person. They obtain their strength either through repetition, intensity or both. Often the lies are not spoken as much as they are implied, so we are not always conscious of them. Lies like this tell us who to be or, in many cases, who *not* to be. They seem so true and the consequences of them seem so potent, they are like steel bands around our heart.

> *"Core lies are the ones that attack or undermine our identity and any attempt to be that person ... Lies like this tell us who to be or, in many cases, who not to be."*

Core lies are strengthened by repetition, the constancy of an experience, because if we hear or see something often enough it eventually seems true. "You are ugly ... Nobody will ever love you ... You will never be safe ... Parents will never take care of you ..." Both words and actions are powerful persuaders.

Core lies are also strengthened by intensity, such as trauma. A single event connected to trauma can bury a lie deeply and firmly in the soul. The loss of a parent, rape, molestation, witnessing violence and many other kinds of traumatic experiences can forcefully imprint upon the soul whatever lie is attached to the event. Two hundred contrary events will not undo the power of a single traumatic event. These core lies attack and undermine who you are, how you view God and your perception of your own value or place in the world. Studying verses about God's protection will not deprogram the lie of a person who has been violated. God Himself must help replace the lie with the truth. The antidote to a lie is not information, it is experiencing the love of the One who is the Truth.

Bad things happen to people. Bad things happen to good people. In no way would I ever suggest that the feelings people have about their circumstances are lies. In fact, one of the most potent lies is when someone states or implies that something painful was not as bad as you thought. Let me state categorically here that when trauma happens or life circumstances are painful, such things are very real. It is what these events imply about your identity or God's nature that I am calling a lie.

SOUL WOUNDS

My friend, Sandy, was constantly shamed in a socially and racially tense classroom. Then she was left in a locked closet in the dark. The fear stayed in her heart like a scar stays with the flesh after an accident. Her mind and emotions suffered deep and long-lasting effects that changed her relationships for decades. Sandy's soul had been wounded.

I use the term *soul wound* to describe the effect of trauma on any part of the soul. The mind, the will and the emotions can all receive trauma and such trauma has an impact on the interaction and integration within the soul. The will may set up defenses to protect the emotions; the mind may try to remove or lower the defenses; but it is double-teamed by the emotions and the will. A wound also provides fertile soil for the lies mentioned above to take root. Because of the intensity of the experience, the lies are more deeply imprinted.

Often the soul works to minimize the pain of these wounds and it may actually prevent real healing from taking place. The will and the mind may bury the intensity of the wound to protect the soul from the immediate pain. But this process does not make the wound better, in fact it only serves to either alter or delay the impact of it. Wounds can take place at any stage of life, and if we do not know how to connect to the One who can heal us, then we try to become our own source for healing. The soul tries to heal the soul, but disconnected from the Source of healing, the soul can only rearrange itself around the wound.

Life Patterns

Sandy lived as if people would soon reject her. The overpowering expectation of shame and fear so impacted her relationships that people did not know how to respond to her. The result was that some did reject her. Commonly called a "self-fulfilling prophecy" the power of the wounds and lies mentioned above means that they compel history to repeat itself.

A life pattern refers to the circular cause and effect of the lies we have lived with. Our pattern of perception, desire, choice, action, experience and impact can feed a lifetime of self-fulfilling prophecy. If it is my perception that I will always be rejected, many of my choices come from that perception. If my choices come from that perception, then my action, experience and relational impact will create a self-fulfilling prophecy. I can get rejected and not know I had anything to do with it. Once this happens, it strengthens the perception that set me up in the first place.

These patterns play themselves out in a variety of contexts. I have seen people leave controlling families and end up in controlling churches. I have seen men leave home, leaving behind their mentally ill mother, and then find themselves married to an emotionally crippled wife. I have seen people somehow end up with jobs or bosses that also repeat a pattern. I am convinced, however, that God originally designed us with an appetite to be restored to wholeness so that we would eventually recognize the wounds and lies that feed the pattern, and turn to Him for restoration. Though it seems like a curse, it would be a greater curse for those wounds to be buried deep in our soul and affect us the rest of our lives. These patterns are clues to the things that are programmed into us by the rule of the kingdom of darkness, our personal history and the makeup of our humanity.

This kind of overview can sound either confusing or overwhelming, and certainly this is not my goal. Nor is my goal to get you to focus on the obstacles mentioned in this chapter. It is my hope to make you aware (but not focused on the fact) that you can sometimes cooperate in your own bondage. But you can, therefore, also cooperate in your own freedom. If you read this chapter and feel that the problems are too confusing or too complex, then go back to the center of the target for this book, namely the key Jesus gave us for life and freedom when He said:

> *"Do not be anxious then, saying 'What shall we eat?' or 'What shall we drink?' or 'With what shall we clothe ourselves?' For all these things the gentiles eagerly seek; for your Heavenly Father knows that you need all these things. But seek first His kingdom and His righteousness and all these things shall be added to you."*

SPIRITUAL OBSTACLES

For thirty years Sandy felt fear; deep, paralyzing fear. It was almost tangible and she said it would just come on her out of nowhere. Along with the fear were the voices. I don't mean the "men in the white coats are on their way" kind of voices. I mean the voices we all "hear" in our heart and in our thoughts: "They hate you ... It's just a matter of time before they find out who you really are ... Who do you think you are anyway, trying to fit in here?"

Everyone seems to hear these voices, but nobody seems to admit it until they are given permission. These voices come with an almost tangible sense of fear, or heaviness, or confusion, depending on what the voices are talking about. Can we give each other permission to talk about this?

The term "spiritual obstacles" does not refer to religious or moral obstacles. It specifically refers to factors within the spiritual realm that may prevent us from becoming who we are. Significant reference has already been made to the spiritual realm, but it is important to make some overt statements. The first obstacle in dealing with the spiritual realm is the simple fact that this realm is invisible: it doesn't lend itself to the ways in which humans perceive and define reality because it cannot be verified by our physical senses.

We live in an intellectual and material society. This does not mean we are smart or wealthy. It simply means that, as "Western" thinking people, our primary channels for defining reality come through observation of the physical or material world and our ability to process cognitively what our senses tell us. Logically thinking men and women have a difficult time really acknowledging, much less acting as if they live in, a world surrounded by invisible forces. Ironically, the same people who are so skeptical of the invisible realm use cell phones, radios and wireless internet without a second thought. Each of these modern conveniences is entirely dependent on the reality of invisible forces in the air. These are forces we cannot see, but each day we act as if interacting with them is perfectly rational. It is our familiarity with these forces that makes radio waves such a helpful metaphor for learning to interact with the spiritual world. We can see the effects of these invisible waves, but we cannot see the waves themselves. It is the same way when dealing with the spiritual realm. We must learn new ways of knowing, and new ways of engaging and interacting with a realm that is foreign to human beings.

Interacting with Invisible Forces

The first principle of interacting with the spiritual realm is "the power of agreement". Understanding this principle will help us a great deal as we learn to overcome obstacles in this area. We see this principle at work in our example of the radio waves that surround us. If we want to tune in to a particular station or improve the reception of a channel we are listening to, how do we do it? What does it take? First, we have to understand that the thing we are after is already present – radio signals are all around us. Second, we have to get our radio to receive and transmit what is already present, which we do by matching frequencies. Each radio station broadcasts on a specific frequency (94.9, 102.7 etc). When our radio receiver matches or *agrees with* that frequency, the signal in the air connects with our receiver. The more precisely the frequency matches, the more powerfully the signal is received. The spiritual realm works in much the same way. *Spiritual forces are empowered by agreement*, like the matching of frequencies that result in a broadcast of information. The way to interact with and empower invisible forces then, is to agree with them. How do we do this? This is where the Bible and specifically Jesus' teaching on the Kingdom is so crucial. Jesus tells us, "The Kingdom of Heaven is like ..." and then gives us a variety of images to illustrate the frequencies of God's Kingdom. When we attune ourselves to these frequencies we agree with and empower the truth of God in our lives.

How does God feel about them?

One of the best examples of the concept of matching frequencies is Jesus' teaching on forgiveness. A significant frequency in the atmosphere of God's kingdom is love. When our heart is turned in any other direction besides love, then we begin to empower the kingdom of darkness in our life. When we forgive, we break an agreement with the kingdom of darkness and restore our agreement with God; we empower His kingdom in our life.

I suppose that God feels one way about people and the devil feels another way. With whom will we agree? Will we allow our opinions and reactions toward a person to be shaped by their behavior or by God's heart toward them? The frequency we tune in to is the one our life will broadcast. If we agree with God and broadcast forgiveness, we have empowered His kingdom within our soul.

Consider then: if we dwell on fear, then fear is empowered in our life, but if we dwell on love, perfect love casts out fear. We must learn how to disengage from the kingdom of darkness and re-engage with God's kingdom of light. What happened to my friend Sandy on the day she became free was that she heard God speak to her heart and He showed her a new picture of her life. When she received love from the Source of love, she agreed with the powerful frequency He was transmitting and it disconnected her from the fear frequency, because "Perfect love casts out all fear." Love and fear are opposite frequencies.

Another way to strengthen our reception is to move closer to the broadcast area. Perhaps you have a wireless router at home for your internet access, so you can move around the house but still stay connected. Though you can receive the signal all over the house, it is at its most concentrated nearest to the router. The further away you go from the router, the less of the signal your computer receives. Similarly, whatever you draw near to empowers one kingdom or the other in your life.

ANOTHER SPIRITUAL OBSTACLE

You will notice a pattern as we address spiritual obstacles. The first obstacle is to overcome the invisibleness of the spiritual realm, as well as our previous *ways* of seeing. Once we see differently, we can deal with the actual problem posed by the obstacle itself. Obstacle number two is the existence of evil. Most of us don't need to be convinced that evil is real and operates in our world today, but we need to be clear that evil is a spiritual entity, not just a bad circumstance. It is easier to defeat something if we know it exists; that is why evil usually operates undercover and its primary weapon is deception. One of the most subtle and destructive deceptions promoted is that evil is not a reality! People buy into this idea: "Yeah, bad stuff happens, but it is just random happenstance and essentially, everything tends toward good." The most difficult enemy to overcome is the one you don't acknowledge exists. Keith Green wrote a song entitled "No One Believes in Me Anymore." It was written as a tongue-in-cheek taunt by the devil and it stated the obvious: he can get away with a lot more if people do not believe in him.

If we know that evil exists in this world and that there is a captain marshalling its forces, then we will prepare ourselves to fight accordingly. If we do not, then we will be overcome by our opponent. The Bible gives us the key to spiritual warfare: we overcome evil with good – not our own idea of goodness, which contains no power, but instead with God's goodness powerfully operating through us. The false assumption that human nature, disconnected from God, is still basically good is detrimental to life on every front, whether applied in the context of raising children or searching for world peace. Palpable evil does exist and it needs to be confronted and resisted.

HOW DO WE CONFRONT AND RESIST EVIL?

Perhaps the most important thing to realize is that we are in a war every day. We need to know this, not so that we will be fearful or anxious, but so we will put on the spiritual armor described in Ephesians 6:10-18. This metaphorical armor symbolizes the very real protection God has provided for ιe midst of the war. Each piece described in this passage enables us to evil and stand our ground. The piece of armor that protects the part of us most vulnerable to the enemy's lies is the "belt" of truth. The enemy fights dirty and strikes some "low blows", but knowing the truth about God and about ourselves will strengthen and protect us. The "breastplate" in the suit of armor symbolizes how being in right relationship with God and others protects us from the enemy's attempts to wound our hearts. We put on the "shoes" God provides for warfare when we prepare ourselves with the good news of His peace before we go to war. This keeps us from being "tripped up" by the enemy's traps, so we can walk through difficult circumstances with God's supernatural peace. This passage instructs us, above all, to lift up our faith in God like a shield, so that we can extinguish all the fiery "missiles" the enemy sends our way. Next in the list of armor is the helmet of Salvation, representing the wholeness, soundness and "aliveness" made available to us through Jesus. When you know you have received the gift of salvation, it acts as a guard over your mind so that the accusing and tormenting thoughts the enemy sends cannot penetrate and destroy you. The last

> *"At the root of any fearful thought is the lie that, somehow, God doesn't love me. When I allow God to expose the lie and show me what the truth is instead, then I can agree with His love for me and the fear will leave."*

piece of armor is actually the one weapon we possess to strike back at the enemy: God's sword. This represents the words He has breathed that we agree with and speak out of our mouths. In fact, in the original language of the Bible it is called a "two-mouthed sword", because when we take the words God has spoken out of His mouth and speak them out of our mouth in agreement and faith, the result of both working together forms a powerful weapon. This is the armor that God has given to enable us to stand against fear, hatred, hopelessness and destruction in all the various ways they manifest in our lives.

We've ALL GOT OUR Demons

"It's only a matter of time before their real feelings win out and they will fire you." Sandy daily drove to work with this nagging "thought" in her mind. This and several other "thoughts" were a constant source of harassment for her. Often, the more she would dwell on them, the louder they became. Isn't it funny how common the phrase, "We've all got our demons" is, and yet if someone starts to take it literally, people react against that idea? The phrase, "He's been dealing with his demons for years" is frequently used referring to addictions or other tormenting struggles that people have not been able to overcome.

Hollywood and religious goofballs have not helped us in this arena. Movies that depict demons tend toward the sensational, showing violent struggles and terrifying spiritual phenomena like objects flying, faces contorting and so on. Even worse, every few months someone shows up in the newspaper having gouged someone's eyes out, or done some bodily damage to them in the name of getting a demon out of them. The thought of violent sessions with lots of squirming or shouting makes people uncomfortable and very reluctant to consider the work of demonic forces in people's lives. Perhaps their discomfort is because the solution often appears worse than whatever caused the need for the session in the first place.

If we are going to trust Jesus as our Teacher and Savior, then we must assume from His experiences that spiritual forces are at work in people's lives. However, do not let other people's experiences or descriptions define for you what that necessarily looks like or what should be done about it. Though Jesus often dealt with demons, those encounters were never His focus. Jesus practiced what He preached. He was seeking first the Kingdom of God and God's way of being and doing right. He assumed that everything else would be added and any obstacle would be removed as He made the first thing the first thing. To Jesus, encounters with demons were minor obstacles to the real mission: proclaiming the Kingdom of God: declaring that God had come to walk among people and reclaim and restore His sons and daughters. Jesus dealt with demonic opposition, but He never went looking for it. He simply disconnected the person from the demonic power so that they could connect with the power of His love and His life.

Encounters with demonic forces should be characterized by a focus on the presence of God and conducted according to the nature of God: love, joy, peace, life and righteousness. As people learn how to empower God's kingdom in their lives and break any agreements they have made with the kingdom of darkness, they are released from the demonic harassment, and it can be a very peaceful release. The overwhelming majority of people I have encountered who have some sort of spiritual obstacle to their freedom experience demonic interference this way: it begins with a persistent or invasive thought, often in their own voice, that begins to accuse or torment. Remember, earlier I described our culture as material and intellectual. Demonic spirits usually find it effective, therefore, to use our own voice against us. We think the thoughts are originating within us, when that is not always the case.

In many cases, people really *are* dealing with their own thoughts. It is normal to have negative, fearful, critical thoughts in a mind that hasn't been used to thinking differently – thinking according to God's perspective. "The natural, sensory-ruled mind is set on death; but the mind of the Spirit is set on life and peace." Fearful thoughts are never the calling card of God's Spirit, but rather the spirit of fear. Keep in mind that spirits are empowered by agreement. This means that if I have fearful thoughts, I might inadvertently invite the spirit of fear to claim some real estate in my mind by agreeing with those thoughts. Instead, I should immediately reject those fearful thoughts by agreeing with the truth. At the root of any fearful thought is the lie that, somehow, God doesn't love me. When I allow God to expose the lie and show me what the truth is instead, then I can agree with His love for me and the fear will leave.

A good way to assess if the voice you are hearing is a spirit other than your own is to observe how you describe it. People often use phrases like, "It just came out of nowhere" or "It just seems to rise up in me." You may want to pay attention to your own descriptions. Another good way to test if what you are hearing is a demonic voice is to assume, for a moment, that it is not your own voice and tell it to stop. The response you get will be helpful in recognizing if this is a thought you are having or a spirit trying to take advantage of your temporary agreement. Recognizing and addressing spiritual forces in your life should not be scary and it should not be done in an overly religious manner. It should be as natural as recognizing that a fly has come into your house and taking the necessary steps to get rid of it.

The real point of learning to recognize and negotiate the spiritual realm is to engage the presence of God, not to get focused on evil and demonic spirits. The fact that I have addressed these things should not lead you to focus on them, just to be aware of them. As a spiritually alive being, your focus and your confidence should be upon your connection to your Creator. As you do that, He will bring to your attention any obstacles He wants to move out of the way. Remember the center of the target: "Seek first the Kingdom of God and His righteousness." He will add to you anything else you need.

Jesus DID NOT Come TO Be SERVED

Jesus spoke our planet into existence and then He came with this simple, powerful and compassionate message: "I know you are trapped. If you also know you are trapped, please realize I am here to help. If you don't think you are trapped, I still have a great deal to offer but you may not want it."

What He did when He physically came to Earth, He still does today: He heals the broken and the broken hearted; He releases prisoners; He gives sight to those who realize they cannot see; and He restores to us the whole-heartedness and wholeness we were created to enjoy. He does for us what we cannot do for ourselves, as we look for His nearness and His answers. He changes our lives by imposing on us a new way to see, not by imposing on us a set of rules by which we should please Him. He looks into our core lies and says: "I love you and I made you just right." He speaks healing into our wounds as we learn to listen. He serves up an atmosphere filled with aliveness, if we will see it around us. He restores our connection to Life and begins to put things in our disintegrated soul back in order.

The point is this: freedom, rightly defined, is the ability to respond to life and to God as the person we were created to be. The first step in that definition is to know that we have become someone other than who we are meant to be. You are stuck being the wrong person until someone else reaches in and rescues you. You cannot become your true self until you encounter the Father and discover that you are His child.

The Father has come back in the person of Jesus. He sees you, wide-eyed, heart uncertain, looking at the things He has placed before you. He has recognized you as His child and invited you back into the family. Having chosen to rejoin your rightful place in the family, He has made all of His resources yours. He will do what you cannot. Sometimes, in a moment, and always during the journey, God, your Father, is speaking to you. He makes the power of His Spirit, the Power of His word and the nearness of His presence available to you. All those things contain the very force that spoke the world into existence and they have the power to restore to you the life for which you were intended.

He can heal your wounds, He can open your eyes; He can tame the rage in your soul and He can climb over every wall you may hide behind in fear. Just by being Himself and being invited to come near, He will help identify and untangle the entanglements of your soul; He will help you become the man or the woman He designed and created you to be. He is here among His people and He is calling you to be yourself.

Chapter 11

Common Entanglements

"Stitched up
Out of my mind, feelin'
Strung out
Laggin' behind, all
Trapped in
Can't do a thing, because I'm
Locked down."
— John Mayer & Herbie Hancock, *Stitched Up*

"There is a feeling like the clenching of a fist
There is a hunger in the center of the chest
There is a passage through the darkness and the mist
And though the body sleeps the heart will never rest.
Shed a little light, O Lord."
— James Taylor, *Shed a Little Light*

"I DON'T have a problem," he growled at me, "my

problem is back in the hospital." He sat across from me in my office, fresh from his father's bedside. In an explosion of mutual fury, this son had bested his father in a fist fight. The suppressed pain of years of abuse had finally erupted as the son sought revenge with every blow to his father's face. With the father in a serious condition, the frightened mother had compelled her son to come to see me; the escalating cycle had to stop. The ensuing conversation revealed that he had not only severely beaten his father, but that he had begun to physically abuse his girlfriend as well. Whether he agreed or not, he had a problem. His mind, will and emotions had become entangled, and his behavior was the evidence.

When our soul becomes dysfunctional, as described in the previous chapter, several predictable conditions arise. If we can recognize these conditions and understand the way to partner with God in untangling our souls, then we can turn the tide and begin to see real and lasting change. This kind of change goes way beyond just behavior management, it actually releases those things that are "not us" which stand in the way of the new us. As we untangle our mind, our will and our emotions, we rediscover the blueprint for our original design and discover that it is easier to become our true selves than it is to continue being the person we thought we were. When we apply the following remedies to the conditions named in this chapter, many of the knots in our soul are untied and it opens the way to become who we really are.

"As we untangle our mind, our will and our emotions, we rediscover the blueprint for our original design and discover that it is easier to become our true selves than it is to continue being the person we thought we were."

Each of these conditions has some things in common: they work *against* us, but they are not intended to do so. Each condition is a misuse or a distortion of something that was intended to work *for* us. Satan is incapable of inventing things. He is not a creator, that is God's role. The only thing the enemy can do is to take things that were intended for our good and turn them against us. Each of the following patterns was designed to help us, yet each one, when distorted, can be used against us.

If you are affected by one or more of these entanglements, you may find it helpful to pray through the prayers included in each section.

Generational Transmission

"I'll never be like my parents!" Uttering this most common declaration is often the first step toward becoming *exactly like* our parents. These words are connected to some inward realities that are already setting our course. While these words belie a number of factors in our mind, will and emotions, they also evidence a fact we all realize: we naturally tend to become like those who raised us. Genetics, learning and relational factors all influence our natural inclination to develop habits, attitudes and beliefs like those who brought us into the world. Like it or not, it is a natural process. We do not have to try.

The Bible even warns us that the things our parents struggled with will influence the things with which we struggle. Our outward evidence of the struggle might be expressed in ways that are different, but it all grows from the same generational root. Specifically, the Bible calls these things "iniquities" and says that they are passed on to three or four generations. An iniquity is a tendency or negative pattern of behavior that we inherited from a family member in a previous generation. Like our DNA, our spiritual makeup also transmits from one generation to another. This phenomenon of generational transmission was originally designed by God to be a good thing. He intended to enable one generation to pass the blessing of its strengths on to the next. However, after the fall, generational transmission became a curse as well as a gift. In addition to broadcasting good traits, bad ones were also transmitted through the family line. We all have a heritage. When we recognize and respond to the effect of that heritage, we take a significant step toward becoming who we are created to be.

It seems unfair that we have certain struggles simply because we were born into a certain heritage, but God mercifully provided a way to reverse the curse of the fall. Jesus explained the way to receive a brand new heritage. He said that our spirit – the essence of who we are – must be *born again*. When we believe and receive what Jesus accomplished for us through His death and resurrection, then we are "born" into a new life and receive a new heritage. Our spirit is instantly changed as it is reconnected to the Source of life. Conversely, the transformation of our soul is progressive and is not automatic. We must consciously reject the harmful tendencies of our previous heritage and yield to the new inclinations God has transmitted into our recreated spirit. We must intentionally lay claim to those things that are true about us now as children of God. As you pray about these things in your life, instead of asking God to help *you* change, agree with Him that He has already changed your source and your heritage. Ask Him to expose and sever the ties to your past that have tried to keep you bound in those generational iniquities. It helps to name them and verbally agree with God that you need Him to break any unhealthy connections that remain from your family. Next, ask Him what is true about you now that you belong to Him.

Pray something like this: "God, please show me anything that has been passed on to me through the generations of my family history."

Now take a moment to listen.

As you know or become aware of things passed down by your family, say out loud, "God, thank you for showing me these things, please sever the connection between me and the source of these issues."

With each thing that comes to mind, ask God to cut the tie to this issue in your family tree. When you believe you have spoken each one of these issues, ask God this question: "God, now that you have made me a new creation, what is true about me now?" As you listen again, speak out loud any of the things that come to your mind. Often the things that come to mind are the opposites of, or replacements for, the things that you have asked God to remove. Speaking them out loud helps you to begin to agree with God and allows Him to work in you.

INNER VOWS AND JUDGMENTS

When we are disconnected from the Spirit of God our soul is left to fend for itself. The executive member of the soul is your *will*. Your will is an important and powerful part of who you are because it is the rudder of your heart. In our earlier discussions, we saw how our will could be used against us if our perceptions were inaccurate. Remember, we make choices based on perceptions and making those choices is the job of our will.

Identity → Perception → Desire → Choice → Action → Experience → Impact

Our will is the most powerful weapon in our arsenal, but we must remember the most important reason why God gave it to us: our will was designed for *submission*. Submission is a word that scares a lot of people because it is so often confused with the word *subjection*, which means to be controlled and dominated by another person or group of people. In contrast, submission refers to the free choice one makes to give themselves to another. If they have not freely chosen to do so (an act of the will), then it is not truly submission. Submission is much more than just allowing God to control your behavior; it is allowing Him to empower your true identity. Your will was given to you so that you might freely give yourself to God's loving rule. He will fix what you cannot.

After the fall of man, however, our disconnected will developed a natural inclination to *push against* – against God, against people, or against anything that appears to constrict or restrain what the soul desires. This is most easily observed in the immediate reactions of most two-year-olds to any parental instruction. With little or no thought, a child will hear an instruction and immediately resist. This is the *easiest* place to see it, but you may notice it in your own heart when someone gives *you* an instruction, asks something of you, or points out an area where you need to change. That resistance you feel coming up inside is the response of your formerly disconnected will.

Now watch this next trap, keeping in mind the *power* of the will and how it is influenced by perception and desire.

I WILL never Go Hungry aGain

Scarlett O'Hara spoke that vow to herself in response to the negative experience she was going through. "I will never …" is a phrase we either declare out loud to others or silently to ourselves. It is a great example of how we make a vow inside our own heart. Based on some experience, our will flexes its muscle and applies its considerable force to try to avoid some predicted pain or discomfort. "I will never be hurt again … I will never go to church again …" We could all fill in the blank. There are countless phrases that our mind speaks to our will to activate a lockdown in our soul, hoping to prevent future painful experiences. Ironically, these inner vows we make to avoid pain often are the very catalysts that produce more pain. "I will never be hurt again" often leads to isolation and loneliness. "I will never go hungry again" can result in compulsive eating and obesity. The list is endless. Carl Jung has said the foundation of all mental illness is the avoidance of legitimate suffering. In all our willful and unconscious attempts to protect ourselves, we sometimes retreat into a not-so-safe world: our own means of protection.

I was a straight "A" student all through high school, yet found myself failing my first two semesters of college. It just seemed harder and less important. Week by week, my grades sank. My mother began to question the value of investing in my lackluster efforts. One day she sat me down and told me her opinion.

"Just because your dad is not paying for this, it's no reason to throw away your college education," she said.

That resistance thing I mentioned earlier? I could feel it rising sharply. In my father's last few years at home, before he left the family, he had inherited a sum of money. It wasn't a fortune, but it would have been enough to cover the college education of my siblings and myself. In the handshake divorce agreement between my parents, he had agreed to use that money to pay for our college. Relieved, I had used my meager savings to purchase an electric guitar. Unfortunately, my father soon found himself in trouble with the law and spent all of the money on his own defense. Since my savings had been depleted, I decided to postpone attending college in the fall in order to work and save money for the spring semester. But when I attended in the spring I performed poorly. The next semester I sat out, once again, and tried to set aside money for the following spring. It was midway through attending that next pitiful semester that the conversation with my mother took place. As she spoke, I argued with her in my mind: "I'm not sabotaging myself because I'm angry at my dad. He can't possibly have that much control over me." But my will had snuck up on me and set itself against my success. It set itself even more firmly when my mother tried to tell me what was happening. She knew what I could not see and my will tried even harder to keep me from seeing the truth when she brought it to my attention.

It took me about a week of stewing before I realized that she was on to something, and another week before I was willing to admit it. Finally I stopped resisting seeing the truth about myself and, more importantly, I stopped trying to "make my dad pay" by failing my classes. Then I enrolled and actually finished my degree with much better grades and no passive-aggressive semesters off. I did not have to submit my will to my mother to get free, I had to submit my will back to God Himself. When I did, I was free to be myself again.

Jesus tells us to be careful how we judge, because we will be judged by the same standard that we use to judge others. When we use our will to judge it is like putting handcuffs on ourselves. If we are not careful, our own judgment of God may make us think that God is small-minded and vengeful, or that if we do something bad, He will "get back" at us. This is not true at all! The if/then instructions God gives us in the Bible are intended to help us to understand just how He designed reality to work. Our perception should be that God wants us to succeed, not that He is trying to threaten us. Jesus was trying to teach us about the limitations we impose on one another.

When we judge someone, we view them through our perceptions and we limit who they are or can be. We look and utter (again, either out loud or in our heart) "There is Bill. He will never amount to anything." Do you hear the limitation we just imposed on Bill? Now listen to Jesus again:

"Be careful of the limitations you impose on others, because those are the same limitations you impose on yourself." When we see someone in a confining, definitive way, our hearts begin to harden based on our perceptions. What is the shape in which our hearts harden? They harden in the image of the judgment we have made. "I will never be like my parents" is a heart-hardening judgment. It sets us on a course to shape our hearts in the very image we are pushing against. If it is their anger I vow to not repeat, then I angrily set my heart. If it is their lack of emotion I set my heart against, then I turn off my heart to protect myself. Again and again, what we harden ourselves *against* becomes the very thing that forms our inner man. In light of that, we can understand that Jesus' instruction, "Be careful how you judge ..." provides both a warning and an explanation about how we are wired.

The question always arises, am I saying that we shouldn't acknowledge that people do wrong things? Is it judgmental to acknowledge that someone is doing something wrong? The attitude of the heart provides the key distinction. If you can discern that someone is doing something wrong, or has a problem, and still express and exhibit God's love toward them, then this is not judgment. It is when you use your discernment to harden your heart that it becomes judgment. Judgment is a choice. If you recognize judgment in your heart, the solution is to stop, acknowledge to God that you have judged someone and stop doing it. Then ask Him to show you that person through *His* eyes, to change any wrong perceptions you may have about them or their motives, and to give you His compassion for them.

As you become aware of these vows and judgments, you must exercise your will again to undo what you did with your will in the beginning. Pray something like this:

"God, I know that I made a vow in my heart, and when I did this I took control of these things in my life ... (be specific here, name the things you have taken control of and the specific vows you may recognize). I see today that you are much better at controlling these things than I am. I am sorry for using my will in this way and damaging my own soul, while leaving you out of this part of my life. Today I choose to renounce this vow or judgment and return control of this part of my life to you. I trust you to do a better job with this part of my life than I have."

FORGIVENESS

Someone has hurt you. I mean really hurt you. You have every right to be angry and you have been for quite a while now. But soon you develop physical pain, maybe in your neck or back, maybe in your guts and the pain becomes chronic. You visit with some well meaning counselor or maybe even a pastor. They ask a few questions and your story comes out. Their diagnosis is that you are hanging on to resentment and you really need to forgive whoever hurt you.

Forgive *them*? Everything in you resists this (sounds familiar, doesn't it?) But forgiving them for this just isn't fair. They really did it; they don't deserve to be forgiven and they haven't apologized or asked for your forgiveness. Besides, isn't it just unfair that the good guys *have to* forgive and the bad guys get away with their stuff?

"Chronic anger and bitterness is one of the most effective strategies to keep you from becoming yourself ... Forgiveness is not a hoop we jump through to make a mad God happy. Instead, it is a gift that allows us to heal from wounds caused by the behavior of others."

Untangling this particular condition is one of the most important steps you can take toward freedom. Chronic anger and bitterness is one of the most effective strategies to keep you from becoming yourself. If God is your Source and you have reconnected to Him, then part of your new nature is love. As I have mentioned a few times, love does not tolerate bad behavior, so this is not what I'm advocating here. But while it is true that love does not tolerate bad behavior, it is equally true that love does not let bad behavior control our heart either. We must be able to remain loving, even as we set whatever boundaries become necessary concerning hurtful or dangerous situations. If God let our behavior change His heart toward us then we would all be in trouble. He may adjust His *responses* toward us, but His heart remains loving because He *is* love. *Forgiveness is not a hoop we jump through to make a mad God happy.* Instead, it is a gift that allows us to heal from wounds caused by the behavior of others and to remain true to God's nature within us in the face of the most horrendous of evils. A few false beliefs about forgiveness may keep people from receiving this most healing of gifts. Let's examine a few of these.

Forgiveness is not *repression.* Repression is when we have painful feelings or experiences and we bury them deeper into our soul, hoping they won't bother us. The problem is that they *do* bother us, just in different ways. The Bible makes it clear, confirmed by scientific proof, that when we hold on to resentment it can have physiological effects. If you swallow poison, it does not prevent the poison from affecting your body, it just determines where the effects will begin: your digestive system. If you swallow the pain caused by other people's behavior, the effects might begin with your digestive system. Many people think that to forgive is to recite a verbal prayer, "I forgive them", and then to swallow the pain others have caused. This is repression and it is not forgiveness.

Forgiveness is not *denial* or *minimization.* To try to convince ourselves that we are okay, or that what happened and how we feel is not as bad as it really is – this is not forgiveness either. The truth sets people free, not self-deception. Jesus did not forgive us by trying to minimize our sin. He called it exactly what it was and still forgave it.

Forgiveness is not *codependency.* This is when we take on responsibility for someone else's behavior and then let them run over us. I think the fear that this will happen keeps many from making the choice to forgive. Let's be clear: the person we forgive is fully responsible for their behavior. To assume their responsibility would not be loving, nor would it be healthy for anyone involved.

SO WHAT IS TRUE FORGIVENESS?

Forgiveness is a two-part process. The first part depends on us; the second and most important part depends on God. When we do our part, it opens the door for God to do His much needed part, freeing us from the hold that other people have over us when we remain resentful. Our part, and I do not want to minimize this, is a *choice*. We choose to move forward in life, carrying the consequences of the other person's sin, and we commit to not charge their sin to their account. Notice I did not say "we carry their sin" though we bear the consequences. As I said before, they are responsible for their sin. But by choosing to forgive, I am saying this: I will live with what they did to me and not hold it against them. I do not want to minimize that this is a very difficult choice and, yes, it is unfair. Just remember, we are not taking responsibility for their sin nor are we excusing it, but we are taking responsibility for what *we do* with their sin. The mental trap we fall into is when we don't want to forgive because we think it is too difficult. But the reality is that we are already enduring the most difficult part: living with what they did to us. It's like the employee who says, "You can't fire me, I quit!" The outcome is the same, they are still without a job; the employee is simply trying to take control of what they do with this painful situation.

"When we choose to forgive we reclaim territory in our own mind. As long as we are holding on to anger toward another, they own real estate in our mind."

The problem we are trying to solve through forgiveness is not the problem of anger. Anger is just a symptom or a secondary response. We are trying to deal with the two things that lie at the root of anger: pain and fear. When someone harms or threatens to harm us, or when they harm someone we care about, the immediate effect is pain or fear, and in many cases both. Anger is simply our way of trying to bring *justice* to the one who harmed us and *healing* to the pain and fear we feel. But to attempt to do away with anger, without getting rid of the roots of pain and fear, is still just repression.

God's part in this process is to cleanse our soul of pain and fear so that we can enjoy the freedom He has provided. The pain and fear can never truly be resolved until we forgive. When we forgive, we receive God's help with the difficult part and that choice produces three immediate and powerful effects.

First, when we choose to forgive we reclaim territory in our own mind. As long as we are holding on to anger toward another, they own real estate in our mind. The more intense the conflict, and the longer the duration, the more acreage they own. People often wonder, in their battle for freedom, why they cannot control their thoughts, or why it is so difficult to control them. Here is the key: you cannot control or give back to God what you do not own. In maintaining resentment, you have given significant parts of your mind over to others, so you will have difficulty controlling your thoughts until you make the difficult choice to forgive.

Second, when we make this choice, we turn the other person over to God for correction. Before they sinned against you, they sinned against God. God is a master of justice and He is able to do more to make things right than we ever can with our misconceptions of justice. Remember when Jesus spoke against the concept of an eye for an eye and a tooth for a tooth? Not only was Jesus trying to prevent us from becoming an eye-less and toothless society, he was trying to help us redefine true justice. Justice is not imposing equal penalties. Justice is when wrong things are made right.

Third, making this choice opens the door for God to heal the roots of pain and fear that have maintained our anger. This is the true goal of forgiveness. Until this restoration process begins, the best we can hope for is to swallow our anger, our pain and our fear – and we have already discussed the danger of this.

Once we make this difficult choice, it allows God to intervene, since He will not override our will. When we peel our fingers back from gripping the wheel in the drive for justice, we experience the weight of the other person's sins being lifted off our shoulders. God is not angry with us, nor stubbornly waiting for us to obey before He will offer to help. Instead, He is keenly aware that we cannot experience healing while we still cling to the source of our pain. So He patiently waits for us to choose. When our will makes the choice, our soul can then access God's supernatural power to forgive, which is available through our recreated spirit. Jesus died on the cross to bear your sins, but He also died to bear the sins committed against you. Forgiving others positions your soul to receive the peace and freedom that Jesus purchased for you by suffering in your place.

EVERYTHING CHANGED IN A DAY

Her father had left them alone with their mother when she was only five years old. Nevertheless, even at this tender age, she was the oldest of four, and due to her mother's instability she began to take on the responsibility of raising her siblings. Mom's meltdowns were sometimes dangerous and left the kids without adult care, so she spent her entire childhood taking care of everyone but herself. In the meantime, her dad began a new family and completely ignored the four kids from his first family.

When I met her, she was in her forties and had endured a series of failed relationships, dealt with bouts of depression and addiction, and was filled with anger against the father who had abandoned her thirty-five years before. About once every decade he had dropped into her life, only to disappear again, fueling her anger and keeping the fire of rage burning. Following our discussion on forgiveness, she fought to genuinely make that difficult choice and not just repeat empty words. When she did speak, the words came from her heart:

"I choose to forgive my father for leaving us alone when we were all little. I forgive him for abandoning my mother and for leaving us in her care when she was unstable. I forgive him for never coming to take care of us and for not loving us ..."

The list went on as she purposed to no longer lay those very real sins to his account. She was in no way saying that he was not responsible, she was simply declaring that she would no longer hold these things against him, waiting for him to somehow change in order for her to be okay. The next part began to relieve her pain:

"God, when he did those things I felt so alone!" She sobbed deeply as she released it to God's healing care. "When he did that I felt scared ..." again, the tears flowed as she released his sins and the years of pain they caused to the One who could really carry them.

"When he left, I felt completely unloved and abandoned," she continued. She was not reciting accusations, she was naming the things she was releasing. One by one the grievous effects of her dad's choices were named, the pain and suffering they had caused were acknowledged, and she released those wounds to Jesus who had been wounded on her behalf. She was receiving healing before my eyes. This was beautiful, but what happened the following week was unbelievable!

She came in the next week and relayed a life-changing story. Without any contact or prompting, and after a decade of absence, her father called the very same week she forgave him. I am convinced that we open the door to miraculous intervention when we stop trying to do God's job. Not only had he called, but he came to visit. He spent a few hours with her and her siblings, then he left. But this time after he left, he called her.

"Something was different this time," he said. "Your brother and sister are still angry with me, I can tell. But you seem … different. Can we get together, just the two of us?"

Her eyes were lit with grateful tears as she described their meeting – how they spent time conversing and interacting, trying to catch up on each other's lives and make up for lost time. Then she summed it all up this way: "Everything I had wanted from him for thirty years we did in one weekend."

For that father and daughter it was the beginning of restoring a relationship. Real justice happened, because something that had been wrong was being made right. No eyes gouged out, no teeth pulled, just right-ness; and it began with her choice to forgive. Forgiveness is not a rigid, uncompassionate demand from a God who does not understand. It is His gift, allowing us to continue to love and maintain a soft heart in the face of real pain and evil.

Pray something like this: "God, today I choose to forgive … (*fill in the name of whoever you are forgiving*) and give them back to you. I will live the rest of my life with what they have done to me and not hold it against them anymore. I forgive them for … (*here, name the specific things they have done that have been hurtful to you*). God, when they did these things to me, I felt … (*here name the feelings that you have been carrying as a result of the harmful actions, or words*). I release these feelings to You now, Lord, and ask that you would bring Your healing touch to my heart."

As you pray through the feelings you have been carrying be mindful of releasing them, trusting that God is willing to carry them for you. Sometimes the emotions will be quite strong as you pray this, but it is important that you release them from your heart and not just name them from your mind. It is your heart that has been carrying these feelings, so feeling the emotions as you pray is normal, and helpful.

Unhealthy Connections

At this point, can you recognize how all the distortions and entanglements within our souls actually reflect the misuse of God-given characteristics? God originally designed and equipped us to live free and fulfilling lives as His children. But the very qualities He designed to be helpful were distorted and turned against us under the bondage of sin. Jesus came to redeem and untangle our souls from sin's destructive impact so that we could live in freedom.

One of God's most amazing attributes is that He can become one with others. When we are born-again we become joined together with Him, restoring our relationship to its original design. God is a connecting "two-become-one" God and He has made us in His image with similar attributes. He designed us to be able to connect and become one with our husband or wife, and even to meaningfully connect with our extended family. We are physical, mental, emotional and spiritual beings who were designed to connect with others on each of those levels, and it is inevitable that we will. However, it is also true that *unhealthy* connections can take place that are outside of God's design. That is when the power of connection works *against* us, not *for* us.

Family relationships are designed to change over time. Parents and siblings are closer at certain times and farther apart at others. By design, there comes a time for a person to leave their parents. This is not just a description of residence, but also of connectedness. Leaving our parents means changing the degree of connectedness to reflect the appropriate stage of life. The level of connectedness for a nursing baby is supposed to be different from the connectedness of a twenty-three year old son. When we fail to negotiate these changes, these connections become unhealthy dependencies. Mental, emotional and even spiritual connections that do not change with time can hinder a person's growth.

Another way a family relationship can cross this line is if a family member is more connected to another than is appropriate for the specific relationship. It is common to find that sometimes children form a closer relationship with a parent than the parents do with one another. This can have destructive effects for the individuals involved as well as for the entire family. It also impacts the generations that follow. The husband and wife are designed to be the most connected relationship in the family. God's design for the family is for the children to grow up and leave home, while the husband and wife remain.

Connections to Others

Sometimes we can make inappropriately close or dependent connections with others such as a boss, a spiritual leader, or even a peer who becomes connected to a closer degree than is appropriate for the nature of your relationship. These connections can impact other relationships and our own development. The most common, most destructive of these inappropriate connections is when we engage in sexual activity with those we are not joined with in a protected, covenant relationship. For years we have watched our nation shift as we debate what we call "moral" issues having to do with cultural values and sexuality. Christians are accused of being prudes and accuse others of being immoral. The debate usually focuses on the issues of disease, pregnancy and morality. If possible, I would like to set those things aside and have a pragmatic discussion about sexual activity from the perspective of one who has helped others untangle knots in their soul in order to discover freedom. In chapter two, we examined a common decoy to freedom: the belief that freedom means living without rules or boundaries. On the contrary, God-inspired boundaries protect our freedom.

Remember our definition of freedom? Freedom is when we can live life fully as the person we are created and restored to be. I want to take a plain and simple look at how sexual activity can either foster this or undermine it. The following is not a true story, but rather an amalgamation of countless stories that I have heard as a counselor over the last twenty years.

A young man or woman comes to my office concerned about some symptoms he or she has been experiencing; not physical, but cognitive or emotional symptoms. They have thoughts that are completely out of the ordinary, such as suicidal or destructive thoughts, or maybe they are experiencing emotional symptoms that are new to them like depression or anxiety. After asking a series of diagnostic questions like, "When did this start?" and "What else was going on in your life at that time?" the stories begin to emerge.

They became involved with someone and then the relationship became physical. Sometimes they engaged in intercourse, but other times they just experienced the intensity of growing sexual feelings as they explored their boundaries. Then comes the surprising part: the things they have been experiencing – the new "symptoms" such as panic attacks, depression or risk-taking behavior – those are characteristic of the person with whom they were involved. What happened? These things are not contagious – at least not in the way we understand contagious. But, again and again, this is what I would hear.

I am convinced that we have approached sexuality as a cultural issue, which is completely backwards. We have asked the question, "What is wrong with it?" and then simply tried to avoid the negative effects of our decision (premature pregnancy, disease, etc). What if, instead, we asked this question: "What is right with sex ... what is it *for?*" I am convinced God gave us sex in order for us to become one with another person. I believe God designed sexual intimacy so that two people, united in marriage and joined together by Him, could express their love for one another and become one flesh –physically, mentally and emotionally. Just because that is not always *our goal* does not mean that it *does not happen.* Two becoming one is not a side effect of sexual activity, it is the purpose of it. The connection that happens at all levels of our being joins us in a profound way. Part of us is deposited deeply in the other person and we carry a part of them inside us as well.

Now, how can we live life as the person we are created to be if we keep giving parts of ourselves away? This is especially the case when we give parts of ourselves to people who go and live separately from us. A part of our heart and soul was connected in sexual activity, whether we intended this to happen or not. If you live in an ongoing relationship of intentional one-ness with that person, then you don't really lose that part, you just share. However, if the sex was just recreational (or part of a temporary relationship) you lose a part of yourself. An equally alarming consequence, illustrated by the counseling scenario I gave, is that you have now *gained* some things you may not have wanted: a part of that person (or persons) has become embedded in your heart and soul. In the context of an ongoing committed relationship we maintain access to one another, sharing ourselves as we share life together, but without that ongoing commitment our soul becomes "fractured".

As we understand the purpose, design and function of our sexuality, we see that the real issue is not what is *wrong* with having sex outside of protected relationships, but rather what is *right* about protecting the heart and soul, not to mention the body, that we have been given. To become the person we are created to be, we must keep all the parts intact and flowing in-sync with the Source of life. The book of Proverbs, an Old Testament book of wisdom, puts it like this: "Keep and guard your heart with all vigilance and above all that you guard, for out of it flow the springs of life." The levels of confusion and dividedness that I have walked people through is a stark indicator of how dangerous it is to misuse the great gift that God has given us in our sexuality.

"Two becoming one is not a side effect of sexual activity, it is the purpose of it."

So what do we do if we have already given away parts of ourselves? What if we are already carrying around aspects of other people from these soul entanglements? Again, we must do something that allows God to do something. This principle is seen again and again in the Bible. When we do our part, God does for us the part that we cannot do. The overall principle of this book is that it is God's nature to restore lost things and to repair broken things. He is happy to do these things for us, but will not force it upon us.

When we realize that we have become divided, or inappropriately connected, we need to tell God that we realize this. Tell Him that you made some choices that have harmed you (and in some cases like rape or incest, you did *not* make any wrong choices, another person did). Tell God you are sorry and that you need His help. Ask Him to break the connections that were formed and to clean out the things that have been deposited in your soul. Last but not least, ask Him to restore to you the things that have been lost from your soul. As you do this, wait quietly and see what He does. I have seen again and again that God loves to restore, loves to heal, loves to make whole and He will do this for you.

As you become aware of connections you may need to break, pray something like this: "God, I admit I have an unhealthy connection with … (*name the person or persons*), and today I need your help to break these connections. I am sorry that I … (*name any choices or actions that you willfully committed that led to these connections*), please forgive me and cleanse me from my role in these connections. Would you please sever the connections that I made with this person (or persons) Lord? Now please show me how you see me separate and cleansed from my connection to this person."

At this time, wait and allow God time to speak to you and show you anything He may want you to see about what He has done in response to this prayer.

CONTACT (OCCULT PRACTICES)

Finally, I would like to look at one other way that we make ourselves vulnerable to bondage. While many other conditions can open us up to deception, confusion and bondage, dealing with the five covered in this section will gain back a great deal of ground. Agree with God about your new heritage and ask Him to cleanse anything from your old heritage that is harming you. Bring your will into submission and recognize specific ways that you may have vowed inwardly things that keep you stuck. Begin to forgive, truly forgive, those who have wronged you. Begin to ask God to reveal and break unhealthy connections to others and especially those that have formed through sexual encounters. You will be amazed at the number of things that change in your life just by untying these common knots in the soul. And last, but not least, let's consider ways that you may have connected to the spiritual world by means other than the one that God Himself has provided.

We are designed to be in an ongoing connection to the spiritual realm. We have discussed that connection throughout these pages. God Himself has made a way for us to be in that life-giving connection to His Spirit. It is central to becoming who we are. God reached across the gap between here and there and invited us to reconnect to His Kingdom. What if we have also been presented with invitations to connect to the spiritual realm that are not from God? What kingdom would we connect with if we responded to those invitations?

There is a material mindset that believes that the human intellect and the physical world is the standard for truth and reality. Then there is another mindset that agrees that a spiritual realm exists, but maintains that we (humans) can come up with multiple ways to connect to it. This produces a variety of schools of thought, each with their own techniques for contacting the spiritual world (i.e. mediums conducting séances, spirit guides and a variety of mystical practices) in order to open the door to another realm. Jesus is the direct connection to God and to the presence and activity of the Holy Spirit and He had a compassionate reason for letting us know that He is the *only way* to enter in. When we try to enter in by any other way, we invite activity from spirits other than God's Holy Spirit. These spirits only intend to harm us. In some cases their influence can seem like a minor annoyance; we could compare it to the debris we pick up as we walk through the woods. Seeds and stickers may cling to our clothing, but can be easily brushed off. In other cases, the effect of these spiritual encounters can be much more intense.

I prayed with a woman one day about this very issue. As soon as I explained it to her, she began to cry. She had been involved with a group in her neighborhood that had been invited to a woman's house for some séances. This woman began to teach them about a variety of ways to contact the spiritual world. It was fun and interesting to them, so all the kids in the neighborhood joined in. About a year into this "fun", one of the kids committed suicide. A few weeks later, another followed suit. A few weeks later, the woman who had been teaching them also took her life. By the time her family moved from the neighborhood, several of the kids had either taken their lives or tried to. She had just pushed this back out of her memory until the day she spoke with me. Jesus said that Satan comes to steal, to kill and to destroy, but that He came to give us abundant life –*aliveness*, as I like to call it. When we prayed, we asked God to remove from her every influence she had opened herself up to and to close any door she had opened through those activities. She felt a tangible sense of relief. She described it as a great weight leaving her body. She felt free because she was! She was experiencing the freedom Jesus came to give her.

The spiritual realm is real. It is a dimension where we can commune with God. He has provided us with a way to cross over and stay in touch with Him through Jesus. Any other way is a counterfeit. If you have engaged in any of the counterfeits named here, or one of hundreds that I did not name, simply admit to God that you have done that, then ask Him to clean from your soul any connections that have been formed by those actions.

When you recognize that you have had contact with the spiritual realm through any means besides God's prescribed method, pray something like this: "God, I confess that I allowed myself to have contact with the spiritual arena by … (*here name the choices or actions by which you contacted the spiritual realm*). I am sorry that I did this. Thank you for forgiving me and cleansing me of any impact of my choices. God, please take from me any residue I may have picked up from my contact with the spiritual realm. I only want to connect through Jesus and through your Holy Spirit. If any spiritual forces gained access to me through my actions, please remove them from my soul."

These five areas: generational transmission, inner vows and judgments, unforgiveness, unhealthy connections, and counterfeit, un-holy spiritual connections are fairly common ways that we fall into the trap of the enemy and get stuck. Thankfully, God loves to restore things to His original design and is just waiting for us to ask.

CHAPTER 12

making all THINGS new

"Behold, I will send you Elijah the prophet ... And he shall turn the heart of the fathers to the children, and the heart of the children to their fathers."

— Malachi the Prophet

"Selah" (pause and let this sink in ...)

— King David of Israel

THIS STORY is not about you. It's not about

me either. It is amazing how much it feels like it is about us and it's not entirely wrong to feel that way. We are so like the One whom it is about and our true nature is so connected to His nature, that the story becomes about us as well. We are not the star, but you cannot tell the story of the Father without it also being about His children. You can't tell the story of the Healer without including those who are healed. And you cannot tell the epic story of the One who takes a broken, deteriorating creation and makes everything new, without telling the story of the renewed at the same time. It *is* about us, since we receive from Him all that is true about Him.

God has been unfolding a plan since long before we were around. His job description is to fill all of creation with His nature. His strategy has always been to do so through you and me. It is His intent that those who have been born from Heaven will be around for the rest of that story. The Kingdom of Heaven is like a certain King who threw a wedding feast for His Son. God is constantly inviting us to rejoin Him in His family. When the story goes on for all of eternity, we will be in it, playing our role and eternally related to the Writer and Star. I don't know how He does it, but He walks what seems to be a tightrope. It is entirely about Him, but in the midst of His own story He comes to us and tells us *our* story matters to Him, along with all of its details. He has preserved our tears in a jar and wept with us. He has numbered our days and the hairs on our head. Meanwhile, He has been steering solar systems throughout the cosmos and He feels no stress.

Somehow, along with our Father, we want to tell our story. As we walk with Him, He writes into our lives the inscription of His nature and our story is part of His. As we are healed, we learn about the Healer. As we are renewed, we get a glimpse of the bigger story of the One who makes all things new. As we become sons and daughters, we progressively learn more about our Father. Our stories are intertwined. We become people whose lives display His story. For us it may be a bit more of a tightrope, but the safety net is wide, since even a great acrobat sometimes falls.

"Right in front of you is the life you have forgotten, so don't back down now."

The Father's story begins and ends with Him. The tightrope for us is to stay humble and not be puffed up, since arrogance is not part of our Father's nature. He cannot help but know that He is the Beginning and the End; yet with all that awareness, His eyes are toward us. He spoke it all into existence and it all returns to Him. It is amazing how our story is not that different. Our life originates with Him, like the infant acrobat began his journey with his *real* parents. And our story can end with Him, though He will never force that upon us. In between our beginning and our end, we are on this earth journey. This journey is the trail upon which His love will eventually ambush us, bringing us to our own acrobat moment: the moment when we might accept His invitation to rejoin His family so we can reclaim our part of the story.

When you join Him in His story, then your story changes forever. The big picture is that you just got the best agent, the best representative, the best advocate – however you want to describe it – your Dad is bigger than, well, anything. But *our* picture is this: I don't feel like His son and on many days I don't conduct myself like I am cut out of the same cloth. I try to change myself. I try to minimize my mistakes and to leverage more and more successes. I see the obstacles and problems on this journey more than I see the big picture and the victorious ending. Because we see from ground level, most of how we think about freedom has to do with trying to overcome obstacles. He quit drinking, now he is free! His anger is gone, freedom!! On and on, as we try to deal with obstacles in our life, we think the next piece of debris must be the one that will finally clear the path to ultimate freedom. The whole focus of our journey can become about removing obstacles, and that would be missing the point. That is why I almost left the chapters on obstacles out of this book! Instead, this is what I'd like us to focus upon:

The young acrobat was free the day he rejoined his real family.
He then became who he was born to be.

Sure, he was untangling the knots in his soul, overcoming doubts and fear, and learning to recognize the lies hidden in his heart. But this was the journey, not the bigger picture. He was back in the family, back in connection with his Source. The real battle had already been won, so everything else was just living out the reality of what happened that day under the big top.

We are all somewhere in the Journey. Perhaps still on the farm, wondering if this is all that life has for us; eyes down, numb inside, having forgotten we were meant for more than the field in front of us. Perhaps we have seen the poster on the wall and felt the fire leap up in our soul, half driving, half teasing us. Maybe we are watching the show, on the edge of our seat, heart in our throats, still not quite sure what is going on, but about to climb out of our own skin from the desire to feel more alive. Perhaps you are one of those wandering around, touching the high bar, rubbing shoulders with those who are doing the very thing that makes your heart scream out loud. You have never done it and don't yet realize that this is your destiny, but it pulls at you like a super magnet! Wake up and reach out. Right in front of you is the life you have forgotten, so don't back down now. Do you feel that

T H I N K   D I F F E R E N T L Y

you are standing between two ways of life? The life you have known is on your left, with all that is familiar and comfortable. You still think this is who you are and everything you know is still connected, in numbing certainty, to life as you have known it. You are looking to your immediate future and it is becoming clear to you right now that life, as you know it, could change. That which has been secure (and yet driving you crazy) seems to be a little less true, and the thing that sets your heart on fire feels astonishingly true, and yet impossible. You have a choice to make.

We live in a time where the pursuit of connecting to God is no longer about church people or non-church people. Right now many lifelong church-goers are reconsidering the way they have pursued God and asking themselves questions like these:

"Is the way I have related to my Father the way He wants to relate to me?"

"Has my church life become a field that I plow out of obligation, not passion?"

"Am I made for something more than the way this is being done?"

The whole landscape of religion is changing on a massive scale and I believe it is not because people are running away from God, it is because they are rediscovering Him outside of the channels traditional religion has prescribed. A good many of us have actually made the leap in recognizing who our true Father is and committing ourselves to the new life with Him. But sometimes, along the path, it becomes difficult. Those who are supposed to be our friends have, in some cases, become a source of pain. Where we should have found support, we found criticism. This is also part of the journey. The barrage of propaganda in the war against our souls has taken its toll in our spiritual communities. We have not known how to help people, so wounded people walk among us. Maybe we *are* the ones who have been wounded by others who have been wounded. Pain propagates pain. Hurting people hurt people.

None of these things change the core truth of our Father's loving pursuit of us and His goodness to restore our soul. None of these things affect His opinion of us. He is just glad to have us back home! He is glad every day that we have come back, and we do not ever need to perform in order to please Him. We must not confuse the diligent pursuit of fulfilling our destiny with some kind of performance upon which God's love or approval hinges.

The story of the human race began with God depositing His nature deeply within us, making us who we are. Then the human race was hijacked through deception and from that point the story unfolded with that one key piece missing. God's nature was still around us but not in us. All the while, He desired to reestablish relationship and again be the one who sustained and maintained us. The separation was destructive to our race as a whole and to each of us individually. God began the reconstruction on both fronts: He is restoring the big picture back to His original design and He also desires to restore you. Removing obstacles is not the essence of freedom. Real freedom is when you can live as the person God created you to be, even in the midst of the journey. He is still restoring you. And He is still restoring me.

TURNING THE HEARTS OF SONS TO THEIR FATHER

I am the youngest of three children and was close to my mother. Things had been unstable for several years and my distant relationship with my father was already deteriorating as he emotionally checked out of the family. The arguments and separation between my parents left us all uncertain about the security of our family.

The best thing we did as a family was our annual camping trip. My dad would take two weeks off every summer and we would load up our Volkswagen and head in a direction, camping our way to and from a variety of destinations. In 1976, when I was fourteen, we took an extra week to make a driving trip through northern Michigan, across Canada and down through the Pacific Northwest. We hiked, skipped rocks, bought snacks at little camp stores and spent time together. It was a memorable time seeing an amazing range of countryside, from the Great Lakes to the Pacific Ocean. We saw the Pacific Northwest and drove back through the Midwest, stopping to see the Salt Flats of Utah. We all had a great time.

And then my dad left.

The trip was barely over when he made his intentions known that he was finished and wanted a divorce. He packed and began a painful process of completely unplugging from our lives. With the smell of fall in the air, for the first time we began school with our family broken. As a young teenager, just discovering himself, I told myself I was okay and just went on. As we picked up the pieces of our shattered home, I swallowed my anger, promising myself I would never be like him. I tried to be helpful and made a few attempts to stay in my father's life, but he clearly was not interested. He had a new life and new women and he just wanted to forget about us.

Two years later, I discovered that God was my Father and He wanted me back in the family. I was surrounded by good people and a few father figures. It was a great beginning to my new life. I had a few friendships, but most would come and go. I considered myself to be more of a loner, so I thought I didn't need friendships – especially from men.

I began to realize some things were not right in my soul and I began the journey of healing. My new life with God and with God's people brought opportunities and understanding which began to replace the pieces of a shattered puzzle. As I let God put my own puzzle back together, I found that it seemed to help others when I shared what I was learning with them. I sensed that this was the thing for which I was born: to help others become whole and free.

I read a variety of books, got a masters degree, and went the route of private practice for several years. During that season, I read everything I could and attended conferences and workshops by many great men and women who had learned from the Lord. They taught from Scripture how to partner with God in the healing process. Several people stood out to me in this crowd; above all, a gentleman named John Sandford. He had pioneered inner healing ministry back when I was still a child. He had founded a ministry called Elijah House and had trained thousands of people around the world. His spiritual mindset and practical knowledge of the human soul made him a major influence on my way of seeing, as well as my approach to helping others.

Then there came a year of great difficulty. Several spiritual fathers had gone the way of my own father; they had given up the fight and left the family. Some of them were close friends, some of them just influential leaders in my life. I was struggling through several difficult things, both professionally and personally, all in a short time. The war for my mind and heart had been intense. My soul was weary and my heart was frayed. I knew I was overdue for a spiritual "tune-up" because I was wondering if I was really cut out for this thing that I once knew, without a doubt, was my calling.

It was in the middle of this season that a good friend mentioned he had a relationship with John Sandford. I asked, with no expectation, if he still did personal counseling. My friend said he would ask and the next day handed me the cell phone number to one of the men I respect most in the world. John Sandford said he would see me.

When I called, John himself picked up the phone, and we worked out a time to get together. He lives in the Pacific Northwest. He told me he would pick me up at the airport and even invited me to stay in his home. I had expected to stay in a nearby hotel, so his offer took me by surprise, but I gladly accepted. During the next few weeks, I mentioned to a few people that I had this trip planned. Most knew John by reputation, but a few did not. When those people asked who he was, here was my stock answer: "John Sandford is the ultimate grandfather of healthy freedom and counseling ministries in the world." Now that may not be everyone's assessment, but it was exactly how I had thought of him for many years.

The time came for my week of counseling and healing. I could never have anticipated what the Lord had in store for me. John picked me up at the airport and drove me directly to his home. Within that loving family, I began to experience much more than counseling and prayer ministry.

"Freedom is not about doing good things and avoiding bad things ... It is the unashamed response to the flame that leaps in your heart when you are near your destiny and your Destiny draws near to you."

John guided me through some very meaningful counseling sessions, but the time in between was equally important and healing to me. We went to the produce market, went to lunch, drove around town, and he talked me through the history of his journey in the ministry of counseling and inner healing. He answered questions and told stories – some with a point, and some just because he was sharing his life with me.

It came time for our last day together and John said he felt strongly that he was to take me up the river. The trip was a long winding drive back up into the mountains and past several campgrounds. He told stories of their family trips up there and he told them as a way of teaching my heart. We stopped at an old camp store and John bought me a Snickers bar. All of this felt so familiar. When we arrived at the campground the gate was closed, so we parked and began to walk in. It was a crisp October morning and we could see our breath. John walked slowly, drawing my attention to a variety of plant life. He ambled through the campground, pointing out spots where his family had spent time together, recalling stories and sharing with me from the overflow of those experiences.

I started to sense something as we walked and I looked over at John, walking quietly down the path beside me. I thought (or heard), "This is how it would have been had my father stayed engaged with the family." We walked on in silence. I had never had an older, more experienced man just walk and share with me like this. It was deeply fathering to my heart.

John took us down to the river. It was a shallow river with a rocky riverbed, bordered by woods on either side. We stood for a moment and then John stooped over slowly. He reached down, picked up a rock and skipped it.

"We used to see who could skip a rock and get it to skip the most times right here," he smiled.

I picked up a rock and he picked up a rock. In one of the most surreal moments of my life, I was skipping rocks with my hero. I got a good one. It had to have skipped seven or eight times! Even though I was a grown man in my forties, I couldn't resist looking over at John. The look in his eyes said, "I'm proud of you." My throat got very thick and I heard, or sensed, these words rise up inside me:

"I will never leave you or forsake you."

I felt the nearness of God. This was not about John, at the moment, it was about my real Father – my Heavenly Father – finding a way to reach me.

Without me expecting it, He showed me a core lie. Subtly, I had always feared God would bail on me, and the fear was especially strong right after good times, because my dad had left right after one of the best times we had ever enjoyed as a family. I didn't even know this lie was there, but now it was out. The wound of an abandoning father had buried this lie deep in my heart and here it was being removed, like surgery.

Then I sensed, as much as heard, "I picked a man you consider to be the ultimate father figure and brought you to a place almost exactly like where the wound began. I gave you this whole week so you would know I am for you and I will always be with you." In that moment my heart began to heal and the power of the lie began to fade. John Sandford was already ten feet down the path, but God had visited me in that riverbed to tell me He knows me and He knows what I need.

The story is not about me and it is not about you. But how can we, the sons and daughters, *not* be in the story? After all, the story is about the Fathering heart of God restoring the hearts of His sons and daughters. Freedom is not about doing good things and avoiding bad things. Freedom is not a matter of removing every last obstacle. Freedom is when you live life as the person you were created and restored to be. It is the unashamed response to the flame that leaps in your heart when you are near your destiny and your Destiny draws near to you. Without *doing* a thing, *becoming* who you are can change those around you and will ultimately be a part of God making all things new.

EPILOGUE

The lights went out. The air was electric with anticipation. The crowd stirred as the spotlight hit the trapeze at the top of the tent on the north end. He stood in the light, aware that everyone was looking, but thinking only of mastering the two things he faced: the trapeze and gravity. The former was now his friend; the latter, his age-old enemy.

The announcer completed the introduction and the acrobat leapt out into the air. The ground was sixty feet below him and the bar of the trapeze was swinging towards him. Suddenly, he was flying. Gravity was his servant, not his master. The fire in him burned freely. He turned in mid-air and caught the bar with one hand. As he twisted, his weight torqued him around his single-handed grip. He spun twice and caught the bar with his other hand in one fluid motion, arcing back toward the other end of the tent. He could hear the audience gasp in delight at his defiance of the natural forces.

The crowd watched with mouths wide open, captivated at what they were seeing. He seemed to be superhuman! As he performed his routine, he summoned all of his skill to push each spin, revolution and arc to the limit. He was good. He was *very* good. But something more than talent and skill came through his performance. The look on his face, the effortless motion, the sheer fluid strength, all of these things screamed one thing. This man was fully alive and living in sheer exultation as he effortlessly conquered this trapeze. He was doing the very thing he was born to do.

On the ground, his father watched. There was no fear, no anger or disappointment, only joy on his face. His son was home at last and he was becoming the man he was born to be. The older acrobat slipped his arm around his wife whose tears were flowing openly. The son they thought they had lost had come home. More than that, he had come alive! Before their eyes, he was becoming everything they had seen in him on the day of his birth.

What was invisible to the human eye was the impact upon those who watched. Hidden in the hearts of little boys and girls, young men and women, and even a few older people, a flame was ignited. They had never seen anything like this before. It was not just the physical performance, they had never seen anyone so *alive*. A fire flickered deep inside many of them. It was like reigniting a great memory of something once cherished but long since forgotten, only they couldn't figure out what it was they had forgotten. They began to experience an awakening in their heart – the realization of something that was true about them. It was not that they themselves were born to be acrobats, but each of them had been created to be someone they had yet to become.

Some went home that day and actually hung swings from the branches of their trees. Others remembered the thing that used to make them feel alive – as alive as the acrobat had appeared to them while performing that day. It wasn't what he had done on the trapeze as much as it was the look on his face and the freedom in his routine. They were all reminded of something they did not know they had forgotten … and that day they began to remember.

ABOUT THE AUTHOR

Bob Hamp is the Executive pastor of Freedom Ministry at Gateway Church in Southlake, Texas. He has spent the last several years designing a unique and meaningful way to help thousands of people experience real freedom from the kinds of things that hold humans captive.

Coming from an unchurched background, he was unexpectedly ambushed by an encounter with God that changed the direction and foundation of his life forever. Licensed as a Professional Counselor in Texas, Bob was in private practice for 16 years, helping people with every type of struggle imaginable. His work with believers and unbelievers alike helped convince him that the message of Jesus contained *real* help for people with *real* problems.

Always looking for unique ways to communicate the power of God's activity among humans, Bob teaches classes and trains pastors in ways to engage people with the living and active God to unleash their God-given identity and purpose.

Bob and his wife Jackee have four grown children each one with their own unique identity and purpose.

For more information about
Bob Hamp and other resources visit

www.bobhamp.com